Word Games

Increase Vocabulary through Fun and

Challenging Games and Puzzles!

Grades 5-6

D0730793

Credits

Author: Kathy Zaun

Production: Quack & Company, Inc.

Illustrations: Kathy Marlin

Cover Design: Peggy Jackson

Printed in the USA • All rights reserved.   ISBN 0-88724-957-4

Table of Contents

Introduction

Word Games is a fun way for students to increase their vocabularies, sharpen their reading skills, and learn some fascinating facts! This book is filled with an exciting variety of games and puzzles that students will enjoy completing. The book features interesting events which occur during the year. The activities complement the events and include specific skills to enhance vocabulary development.

Solving crossword puzzles and word searches, completing analogies, and unscrambling words are just a few of the stimulating types of word-based activities students complete in this book. All words are grade-appropriate, and the activities are sure to improve a variety of language skills. Students can work individually or in small groups to complete these challenging activities.

Whether you want to improve students' vocabulary skills or just provide them with meaningful and stimulating word-based activities, *Word Games* is sure to delight and captivate all who complete its pages.

Get Your Paper Here!

Barney Flaherty became America's first paperboy when he answered an ad and agreed to buy and resell newspapers. Newspaper Carrier Day, September 4, honors this industrious boy and all newspaper carriers.

To find out the answers to two questions about Barney, write a homophone for each word. Then, read the boxed letters in order to answer each question.

What newspaper did Barney sell?

1. need ___ ___ ___ ___ ___
2. cereal ___ ___ ___ ___ ___ ___
3. would ___ ___ ___ ___ ___
4. ewe ___ ___ ___
5. grown ___ ___ ___ ___ ___ ___
6. alter ___ ___ ___ ___ ___ ___
7. break ___ ___ ___ ___ ___
8. guest ___ ___ ___ ___ ___ ___
9. poor ___ ___ ___ ___
10. nose ___ ___ ___ ___ ___

How old was Barney when he became the first paperboy?

11. chance ___ ___ ___ ___ ___ ___
12. find ___ ___ ___ ___ ___ ___
13. earn ___ ___ ___ ___
14. fairy ___ ___ ___ ___ ___
15. hole ___ ___ ___ ___
16. plain ___ ___ ___ ___ ___
17. deer ___ ___ ___ ___
18. cellar ___ ___ ___ ___ ___ ___ ___
19. allowed ___ ___ ___ ___ ___ ___
20. chilly ___ ___ ___ ___ ___ ___
21. board ___ ___ ___ ___ ___

Name _____

Wonderful Workers

Labor Day is celebrated on the first Monday in September. This holiday honors all working people. Do you know where this legal holiday is observed?

To find out, read each clue. Write the answers in the puzzles. When the puzzles are complete, write the first letter from each answer in order on the blanks at the bottom of the page.

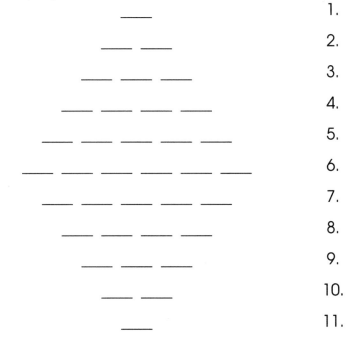

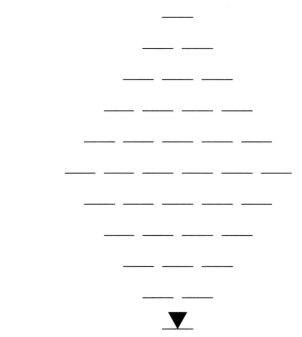

1. last vowel in the alphabet
2. a word that has the same meaning in every language
3. synonym for *sick*
4. past tense for *tell*
5. antonym for *full*
6. to ask for with authority
7. homophone for *steal*
8. a job or duty someone must complete
9. word used to show connection or addition
10. abbreviation for *toilet paper*
11. second vowel in the alphabet

1. nineteenth letter of the alphabet
2. abbreviation for *Alabama*
3. homophone for *knew*
4. antonym for *light*
5. sugar treat
6. to appoint someone
7. having to do with the nose
8. slightly open
9. not bright or clear; low light
10. the time from midnight to noon

___ ___

Be Nice and Polite

September is National Courtesy Month.

Read the clues to solve the puzzle. Clues with an * next to them relate to the word *courtesy*. Clues without an * might apply to someone who is not very courteous. To answer the question, unscramble the circled letters.

What famous American song was written by Francis Scott Key on September 14, 1814?

" ___ ___ ___   ___ ___ ___ ___ - ___ ___ ___ ___ ___ ___ ___   ___ ___ ___ ___ ___ ___ "

Across

2. to agree or pledge to do or not do something*
4. doing what is asked or told*
8. willing to recognize and respect the beliefs and ways of others, even if different from yours*
9. showing thanks*
11. to forgive*
12. to be assertive; hostile

Down

1. savage; fierce
2. able to wait without complaining*
3. to give help or approval*
5. unfriendly; showing dislike
6. to feel hate or disgust for
7. to annoy or make angry
10. cruel; unfriendly

Space Talk

On September 12, 1959, Russians launched the first rocket to the moon. Many more exciting advancements in space have been achieved since that day!

Use the clues and the letters in the space vehicles' names to determine the words.

1. Space probes have visited every planet but Pluto. They provide us with fascinating information about the planets. One space probe is *Pathfinder*.

   a. a person you know well and like ◯ __ __ __ __ __

   b. stone or brick floor of a fireplace __ __ __ __ __ __

   c. to hold back __ ◯ __ __ __ __

   d. to make empty or dry __ __ __ __ __

   e. dad ◯ __ ◯ __ __ __

2. Space shuttles are spacecraft that can be used again. The first one, *Columbia*, took off in 1981.

   a. to declare as one's own __ __ __ __ __

   b. homophone for *male* __ __ __ __

   c. a young sheep __ __ __ __

   d. to go up using feet and hands __ __ __ __ __

3. In 1986, the space shuttle *Challenger* exploded. Frost had weakened seals on its fuel tank.

   a. to make different __ __ __ __ __ ◯

   b. color of grass __ __ ◯ __ ◯

   c. back part of the foot __ __ __ __

      and its homophone __ __ __ __

   d. what the ear is used for __ __ __ __

      and its homophone __ __ __ __

Write the circled letters in order to complete the sentence.

An astronaut who orbits Earth can see the sun rise and

set __ __ __ __ __ __ __ times a day.

Name _____

Sign on the Dotted Line

Constitution Week, September 17–23, celebrates the signing of the Constitution of the United States on September 17, 1787.

Circle the words from the Word Bank in the puzzle. Each word relates to this famous document. Then, write the uncircled letters in order to answer the questions. Words appear horizontally, vertically, and diagonally.

Word Bank

document
preserve
accurate
controversial
significant
extraordinary
effective
independence
substantial
steadfast
survive
extensive
inspiring
celebrate
triumph
enduring

i	n	d	e	p	e	n	d	e	n	c	e	g	e	l
o	r	e	t	a	r	b	e	l	e	c	g	h	s	a
e	e	v	i	s	n	e	t	x	e	w	p	u	a	i
s	e	h	i	n	g	t	o	n	j	m	b	a	g	s
m	v	e	s	e	v	i	v	r	u	s	t	m	n	r
i	r	a	d	i	s	o	n	i	t	j	n	a	i	e
n	e	m	e	s	m	a	r	a	d	i	e	s	r	v
s	s	o	n	r	h	t	n	o	d	e	m	i	u	o
p	e	f	f	e	c	t	i	v	e	s	u	l	d	r
i	r	a	n	s	i	g	n	i	f	i	c	a	n	t
r	p	d	n	a	d	i	b	c	s	h	o	r	e	n
i	f	r	l	g	o	w	e	i	t	n	d	f	v	o
n	d	t	l	h	a	c	c	u	r	a	t	e	g	c
g	t	s	a	f	d	a	e	t	s	p	h	p	o	s
e	x	t	r	a	o	r	d	i	n	a	r	y	e	r

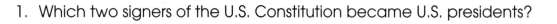

1. Which two signers of the U.S. Constitution became U.S. presidents?

_____ and _____

2. Who is called the "Father of the Constitution?" _____

3. Which state did not send any representatives to the constitutional convention? _____

Name _____

Good-Bye Summer, Hello Fall

Summer ends and autumn begins on September 22 or 23 with the autumnal equinox. This is one of the two times a year when the sun is exactly above the equator, and night and day are both 12 hours long all over the earth.

All but six of the words below relate to the four seasons. Write each word under the correct season and cross it off. Write the six remaining words in the correct order to learn about the origin of *equinox*.

Equinox comes from the _____ _____

_____ " _____ " _____ " _____ . "

seedtime	night	February	vacation
Hanukkah	mosquitoes	sweltering	sprout
October	blizzard	words	fireworks
watermelon	independence	bonfires	autumn
equal	November	July	for
crisp	Latin	Christmas	Halloween
snowflake	Thanksgiving	windy	frigid
August	avalanche	April	May
Kwanzaa	showers	and	bloom

Winter	Spring	Summer	Fall

Name _____

What's in a Word?

The word *September* comes from the Latin word *Septem*, meaning *seven*. September was originally the seventh month of the year.

The only vowel in *September* and in its origin and meaning is *e*. Each word puzzle features the letter *e*. Read the clues. Add one letter to each word up to the fifth clue. Then, remove one letter until only *e* is left. The letters can be in any order.

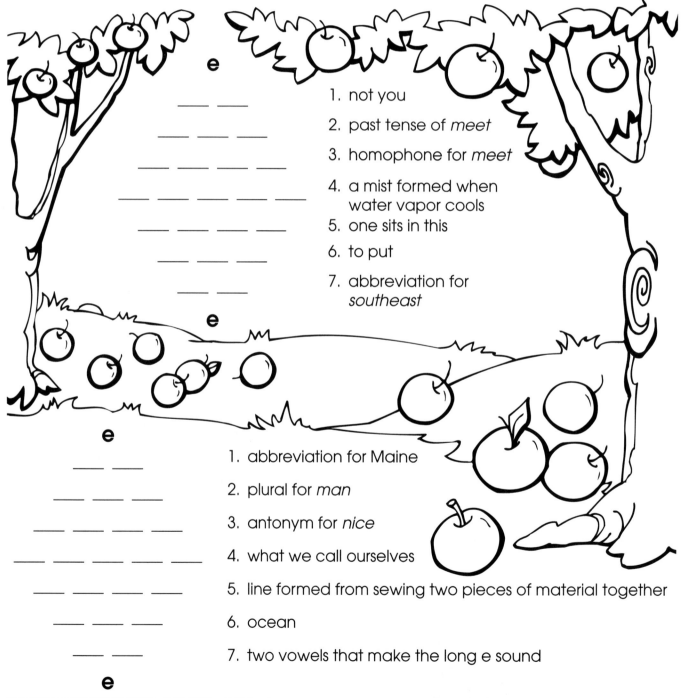

e

___ ___

___ ___ ___

___ ___ ___ ___

___ ___ ___ ___ ___

___ ___ ___ ___

___ ___ ___

___ ___

e

1. not you
2. past tense of *meet*
3. homophone for *meet*
4. a mist formed when water vapor cools
5. one sits in this
6. to put
7. abbreviation for *southeast*

e

___ ___

___ ___ ___

___ ___ ___ ___

___ ___ ___ ___ ___

___ ___ ___ ___

___ ___ ___

___ ___

e

1. abbreviation for Maine
2. plural for *man*
3. antonym for *nice*
4. what we call ourselves
5. line formed from sewing two pieces of material together
6. ocean
7. two vowels that make the long e sound

Apples for Everyone

American pioneer Johnny Appleseed was born on September 26.

To find out his real name, write an antonym for each word in the boxes. Then, use the number code to fill in the blanks below.

cheap ☐☐☐☐☐☐☐☐☐
         8   4

superior ☐☐☐☐☐☐☐☐
          11   2

guilty ☐☐☐☐☐☐☐
        11 4 2 5   11

leader ☐☐☐☐☐☐☐
         2   2

straight ☐☐☐☐☐☐
          5   2 2

unusual ☐☐☐☐☐☐☐☐
          2   4 10

valuable ☐☐☐☐☐☐☐☐☐
           2   3

stingy ☐☐☐☐☐☐☐☐
         11   2

temporary ☐☐☐☐☐☐☐☐☐
            8   9 7 4   11

grumpy ☐☐☐☐☐☐
          1 2

solid ☐☐☐☐☐☐

light ☐☐☐☐☐
        3   7

late ☐☐☐☐☐
          10

smooth ☐☐☐☐☐
          2   6

save ☐☐☐☐☐
        8   11

common ☐☐☐☐☐
            7

silent ☐☐☐☐☐
        4 2

___ ___ ___ ___   ___ ___ ___ ___ ___ ___ ___
 1   2   3   4   5   6   7   8   9   10 11

Grab a Book and Read

September is International Literacy Month.

To answer the riddle below, complete each puzzle. The first two letters for each word are given. Decide which two two-letter fragments will complete each word. Each fragment can be used only once. Then, use the number code to fill in the blanks below.

ks	im	ys	lo	ct	ce	er
la	re	ib	su	le	et	ay
rd	mb	un	on	ny	ea	

1. | a | b | | |₁₁| | | — 1. silly

2. | c | r | |₂|₉| |₁₂| | — 2. used in coloring

3. | b | o | |₁₃| | |₁| | — 3. jump

4. | v | i | | |₅| | | — 4. a person who is cheated or wronged

5. | s | t | | | |₁₄| | — 5. road

6. | d | e | | |₆| | | — 6. periods of time in which things are late

7. | s | t | | | |₇| | — 7. big slices of meat

8. | l | u | | | |₈| | — 8. wood

9. | c | o | |₁₀| |₃| | — 9. a group of animals living together

10. | e | d |₄| | | | | — 10. able to be eaten

What did the book say to the librarian?

___ ___ ___ ___ ___ ___ ___ ___ ___ ___ ___ ___ ___ ___ ?
1 2 3   4   5 6 7 8   9 10 11   12 13 14

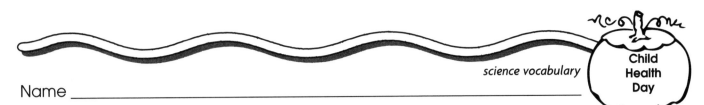

Name _____

Stay Healthy

Child Health Day, the first Monday in October, emphasizes the importance of physical and mental health for children. One way to stay healthy is to eat right. Do you know about how much the food a person eats in a year weighs?

To find out, use the clues about body parts to complete each puzzle. Some scrambled words have been provided. Then, write the circled letters in order on the blanks to answer the question.

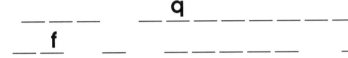

___ ___ ___   ___ q ___ ___ ___ ___ ___ ___ ___

___ f ___   ___   ___ ___ ___ ___ ___   ___ ___ ___

1. carries blood away from the heart—*retyra*

2. seen a lot on Valentine's Day

3. homophone for *vane*

4. remove water and waste from blood to bladder—*yiednks*

5. protects the brain

6. covers your body

7. carry messages to and from brain—*seenrv*

8. center of thought, memory, and feelings

9. framework of bones

10. two masses of tissue at back of mouth— *snotsli*

11. clear, liquid part of blood—*smalpa*

12. used for breathing—*snugl*

13. helps break down food into substances the body can absorb—*reliv*

14. working out makes these strong

15. fills center of most bones

Name _____

A Great Explorer

The second Monday in October is set aside as a day to honor the great explorer Christopher Columbus. It recognizes his landing in America on October 12, 1492.

The word *explorer* contains the prefix *ex-*, meaning *out, from,* or *beyond.* Other prefixes include *il-, in-, ir-,* and *un-,* meaning *not; re-,* meaning *again;* and *pre-,* meaning *before.*

Write the correct word using the clues and prefixes to learn what increased exploration on October 26, 1825. Write the letters in the boxes in order on the blanks.

— — — —   — — — —

— — — — — — — — __ to traffic

ex-	1.	breathe out
	2.	put into words
	3.	died out
il-	4.	not able to read
re-	5.	to remember
	6.	move to a new place
un-	7.	not smart
	8.	not ordinary
in-	9.	not near a coast
	10.	not true
pre-	11.	before history was written
	12.	tell what will happen in future
ir-	13.	not showing a sense of duty
	14.	not able to be changed
	15.	not redeemable

Name _____

vocabulary   **Earth Science Week**

Earth Science Week Is Here!

The second full week in October is dedicated to helping people realize the importance of learning about Earth and its properties.

Write the answer to each clue in the puzzle. Then, write the outside letters in numerical order to answer the question below.

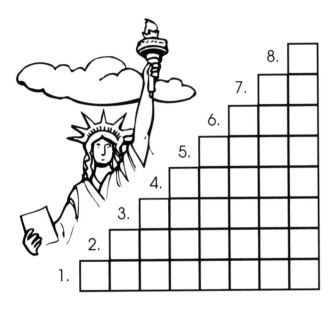

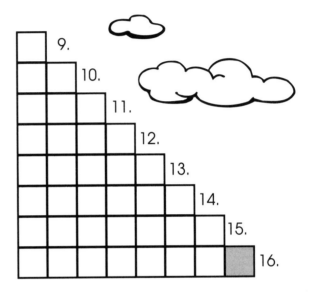

1. set apart

2. a whirling, destructive funnel of air

3. response

4. weary

5. a part of a school course

6. female sheep

7. antonym for *off*

8.–9. postal code for Florida

10. third note of a musical scale

11. record of money owed

12. curving ridge of water on a sea or ocean

13. a natural stream of water that flows into another large stream

14. past tense of *buy*

15. closest planet to the sun

16. 60 in an hour

Tsunamis are huge waves triggered by earthquakes. The tallest one on record appeared in 1971 near Japan. It was almost as tall as a famous American landmark that was dedicated on October 28, 1886. What is the landmark?

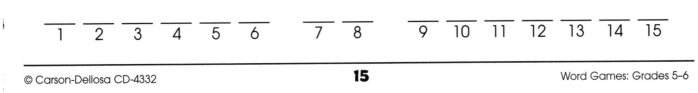

___ ___ ___ ___ ___ ___ ___ ___ ___ ___ ___ ___ ___ ___ ___
 1   2   3   4   5   6   7   8   9 10 11 12 13 14 15

Name _____

"O" for October

October comes from the Latin word *Octobris,* meaning *eight.* Originally, it was the eighth month of the year. October begins with the letter *o.* Each word puzzle features the letter *o.* Add one letter to each word up to the fifth clue. Then, remove one letter until only *o* is left. The letters can be in any order.

O

— —

— — —

— — — —

— — — — —

— — — —

— — —

— —

1. homophone for *too*
2. to decay
3. what a horse does
4. furry animal with webbed feet for swimming
5. to carry in arms or on back
6. young child
7. abbreviation for *Old Testament*

O

O

— —

— — —

— — — —

— — — — —

— — — —

— — —

— —

1. therefore
2. male offspring
3. found in the middle of the face
4. a rock
5. a musical tone
6. in no way
7. a universal word

O

O

— —

— — —

— — — —

— — — — —

— — — —

— — —

— —

1. an interjection
2. antonym for *cold*
3. past tense of *shoot*
4. done with a basketball
5. what an owl does
6. also
7. a preposition

O

Name _____

A Wordy Wonder

Someone very interested in words was born on October 16, 1758. His birthday is celebrated with his own special day. To find out who he was, use a dictionary to write the meaning of each suffix listed. Use the clues and the correct suffixes to write new words. Some letters have been given. Then, write the letters from the shaded boxes in order on the blanks.

-ness — _____

-ous — _____

-able — _____

-ly — _____

1. able to be inflated   ___ ▢ ___ ___ ___ ___ ___ ___ ___ ___

2. able to be recognized   ___ ___ ___ ▢ ___ ___ ___ ___ ___ ___ ___ ___

3. synonym for *tiredness*   **w** ___ ___ ▢ ___ ___ ___ ___ ___

4. with joy   ▢ ___ **p** ___ ___ ___ ___

5. marvelous; miraculous   ▢ ___ ___ **d** ___ ___ ___

6. with sameness   ▢ **q** ___ ___ ___ ___ ___

7. incredible; awesome   **f** ___ ▢ ___ ___ ___ ___

8. capable of killing by poison   **p** ___ ___ ___ ▢ ___ ___ ___

9. having no end   **c** ___ ___ ▢ ___ ___ ___ ___

10. able to be broken   **b** ___ ___ ▢ ___ ___ ___

11. huge; gigantic   **e** ___ ___ ▢ ___ ___ ___

Dictionary Day, October 16, 1758, is a special day honoring

___ ___ ___ ___ ___   ___ ___ ___ ___ ___ ___ ___ ___ ___'s birthday.

United
Nations
Day

Name _____

Peace on Earth

The United Nations was created after World War II to help countries develop positive relationships with each other. It promotes world peace and security and encourages countries to work together to solve international problems. October 24 honors this organization that was founded in 1945.

Circle the names of some of the countries that belong to this organization in the puzzle. The words appear horizontally, vertically, and diagonally.

Word Bank

Algeria	Denmark	Haiti	Lebanon	Poland
Argentina	Djibouti	India	Mali	Senegal
Australia	Ecuador	Ireland	Mexico	Somalia
Belgium	Egypt	Japan	Niger	Thailand
Belize	Fiji	Kenya	Norway	United States
Canada	Greece	Kuwait	Oman	Zaire
Cuba	Granada	Laos	Peru	Zambia

```
L B U K G R A N A D A O P E R U I U
N E I U H T E A D N M A R T I J R N
O L B W N A S U N A E I N D I A E I
W G Y A O R I S N K A C C I P P L T
T I Y I N F I T N Z L U A O N A A E
Z U F T D O Z R I M N B L X M N N D
A M I P N D N A Y N Y A W R O N D S
M O J L S T G L K E N Y A O C I O T
B B I T U O B I J D L A O S I G T A
I E L A E T C A N A D A P R X E S T
A G L T H A I L A N D E C E E R G E
O Y Y I R R O D A U C E G B M S T S
L P O B Z G E S E N E G A L I N D I
P T N K D E N M A R K A I R E G L A
S O M A L I A K G A N I T N E G R A
```

Name _____

Pizza Pie Time

October is National Pizza Month. It celebrates the birth of this delicious treat that was invented in 1889 by Italian baker Raffael Espesito.

Pizza and *mozzarella* contain double letters. Write a double-letter word for each clue.

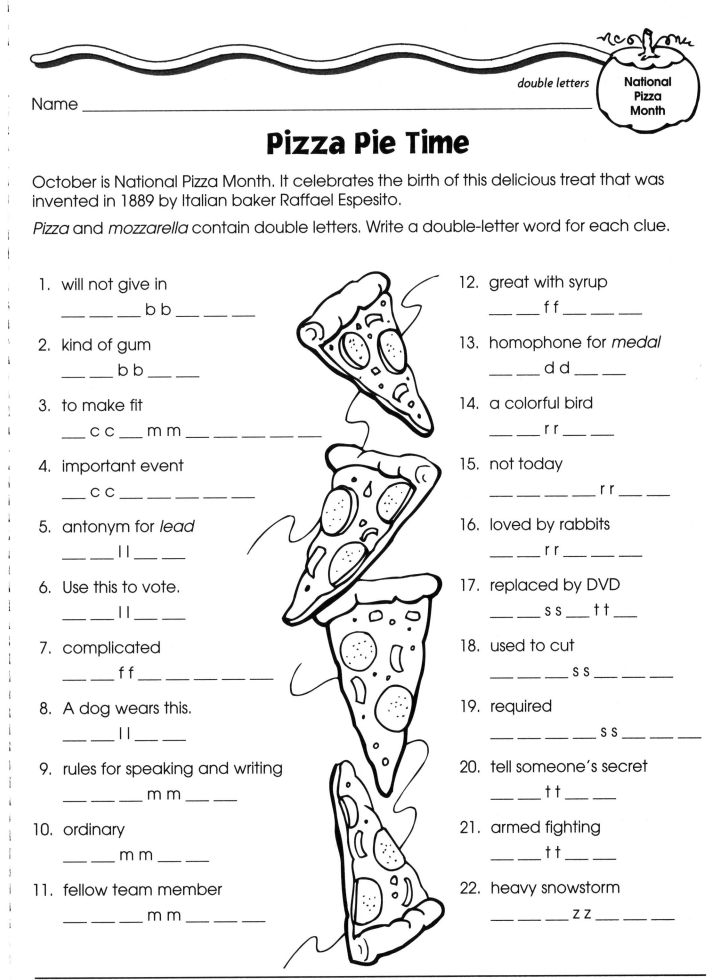

1. will not give in
   __ __ __ b b __ __ __

2. kind of gum
   __ __ b b __ __

3. to make fit
   __ c c __ m m __ __ __ __ __

4. important event
   __ c c __ __ __ __ __

5. antonym for *lead*
   __ __ l l __ __

6. Use this to vote.
   __ __ l l __ __

7. complicated
   __ __ f f __ __ __ __ __

8. A dog wears this.
   __ __ l l __ __

9. rules for speaking and writing
   __ __ __ m m __ __

10. ordinary
    __ __ m m __ __

11. fellow team member
    __ __ __ m m __ __

12. great with syrup
    __ __ f f __ __ __

13. homophone for *medal*
    __ __ d d __ __

14. a colorful bird
    __ __ r r __ __

15. not today
    __ __ __ __ r r __ __

16. loved by rabbits
    __ __ r r __ __ __

17. replaced by DVD
    __ __ s s __ t t __

18. used to cut
    __ __ __ s s __ __ __

19. required
    __ __ __ __ s s __ __

20. tell someone's secret
    __ __ t t __ __

21. armed fighting
    __ __ t t __ __

22. heavy snowstorm
    __ __ __ z z __ __ __

Name _____

suffixes -ant and -ent

John Adams's Birthday

What a Day!

John Adams was born on October 30, 1735. He was the second president of the United States. Adams and another president died on July 4, 1826, on the 50th anniversary of the signing of an important document.

President ends with the suffix *-ent*. Write a new word ending in *-ent* or *-ant* for each word below to determine which president died on the same day as Adams.

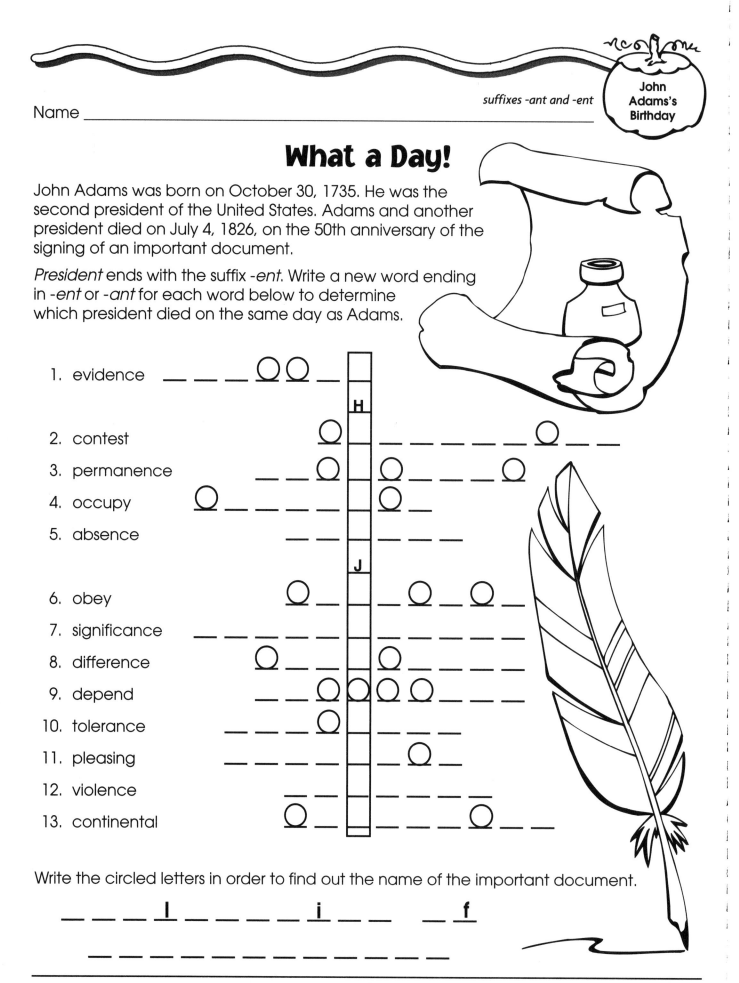

1. evidence
2. contest
3. permanence
4. occupy
5. absence
6. obey
7. significance
8. difference
9. depend
10. tolerance
11. pleasing
12. violence
13. continental

Write the circled letters in order to find out the name of the important document.

_ _ _ _ l _ _ _ _ _ i _ _ _ _ f _

_ _ _ _ _ _ _ _ _ _ _ _ _

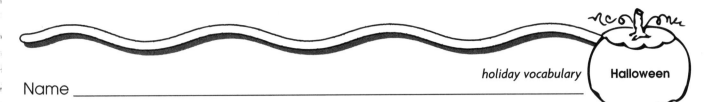

Name _____

Costumes and Candy

Always celebrated on October 31, this ancient holiday has become a time to create imaginative costumes, carve pumpkins, and be a part of fun parties.

Complete the puzzle with words relating to Halloween. The letters in *Halloween* have been provided.

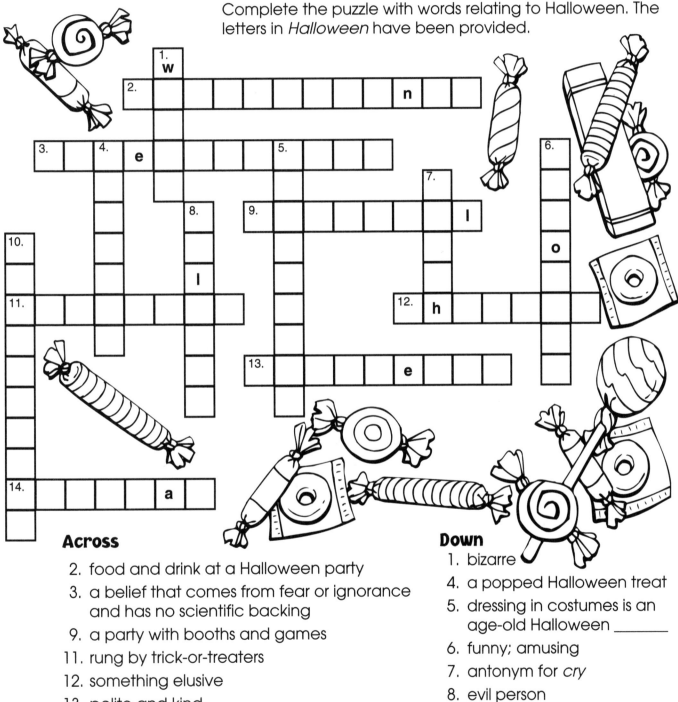

Across

2. food and drink at a Halloween party
3. a belief that comes from fear or ignorance and has no scientific backing
9. a party with booths and games
11. rung by trick-or-treaters
12. something elusive
13. polite and kind
14. not ordinary

Down

1. bizarre
4. a popped Halloween treat
5. dressing in costumes is an age-old Halloween _____
6. funny; amusing
7. antonym for *cry*
8. evil person
10. foolish; absurd

Name _____

Go Vote!

Every vote counts! That is why it is important for every eligible person to exercise his right to vote. This is especially important on General Election Day, the Tuesday after the first Monday in November.

Write a word that ends with -ion in the boxes for each clue. Then, write the letters from the shaded boxes in order to finish the names of men who were voted to be president. Each one was born in November.

1. act of hallucinating
2. something located
3. advance in position or job
4. in-depth talk
5. north, south, east, west
6. idea
7. something suggested

Warren G. __ __ __ __ __ __ __ __ (11/2/1865)

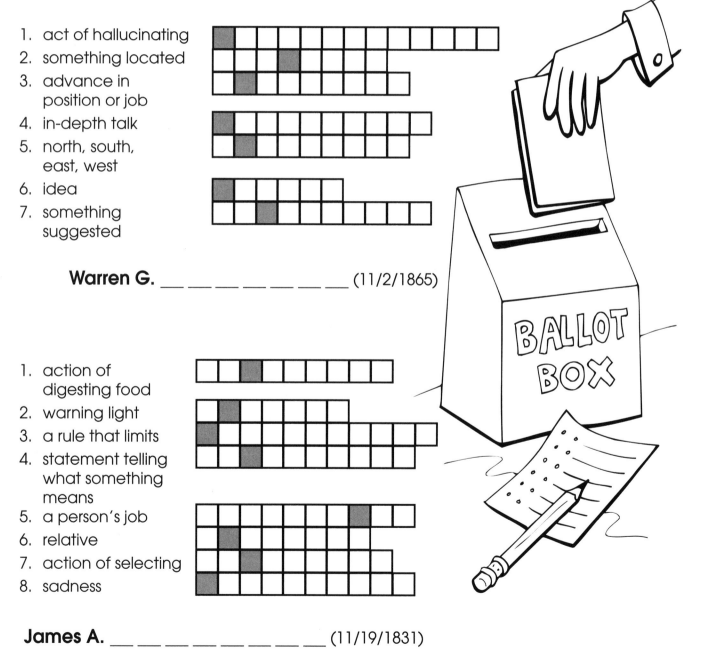

1. action of digesting food
2. warning light
3. a rule that limits
4. statement telling what something means
5. a person's job
6. relative
7. action of selecting
8. sadness

James A. __ __ __ __ __ __ __ __ __ (11/19/1831)

Far Out!

Edmond Halley was born on November 8, 1656. This English astronomer is recognized for his work on comets, particularly the one that bears his name.

Circle the space-related words from the Word Bank in the puzzle. The words appear horizontally, vertically, and diagonally.

Word Bank

galaxy	black hole	comet	Halley's comet
revolves	quasar	asteroid	meteorite
telescope	orbit	nebula	meteoroid
space	light-year	atmosphere	constellation
meteor	astronomy	elliptical	supernova

```
p  t  s  r  o  d  x  a  r  e  v  o  l  v  e  s
g  e  r  d  o  z  l  m  i  m  l  e  s  r  w  y
g  l  b  l  i  g  h  t  y  e  a  r  w  w  w  w
a  e  m  q  u  a  s  a  r  t  b  k  a  f  e  o
l  s  e  v  r  l  u  t  m  e  p  s  l  h  l  r
a  c  t  c  v  u  o  e  l  o  h  k  c  a  l  b
x  o  e  r  a  b  g  e  w  r  w  o  w  s  i  i
y  p  o  b  o  e  r  a  a  g  m  d  e  t  p  t
o  e  r  f  a  n  s  v  s  e  o  r  t  e  t  s
s  n  i  o  t  e  o  v  t  i  f  y  t  r  i  p
o  r  t  e  t  n  h  m  a  n  f  i  f  o  c  a
m  d  e  n  r  a  s  e  y  l  c  i  h  i  a  c
r  v  x  e  r  e  h  p  s  o  m  t  a  d  l  e
e  v  p  o  r  r  d  i  o  r  o  e  t  e  m  n
l  u  u  c  o  n  s  t  e  l  l  a  t  i  o  n
s  x  i  t  e  m  o  c  s  y  e  l  l  a  h  s
```

Name _____

Watch for Falling Meteorites

In November 1954, a meteorite fell through the roof of Elizabeth Hodge's home in Sylacauyu, Alabama, striking her on the hip! A meteorite is a piece of rock and metal that falls from the asteroid belt, from Mars, or the moon. An asteroid is a rocky object that revolves around the sun.

Use the letters in *meteorite* and *asteroid* to write a word for each clue.

meteorite

1. a pest that eats wood _ _ _ _ _ _ _
2. homophone for *meat* _ _ _ _ _
3. to leave out _ _ _ _
4. a carved pole _ _ _ _ _
5. to cut or clip _ _ _ _
6. to become weary _ _ _ _
7. homophone for *wrote* _ _ _ _
8. system of measuring the passing of hours _ _ _ _
9. division of a school year _ _ _ _
10. to carry in the arms or on the back _ _ _ _

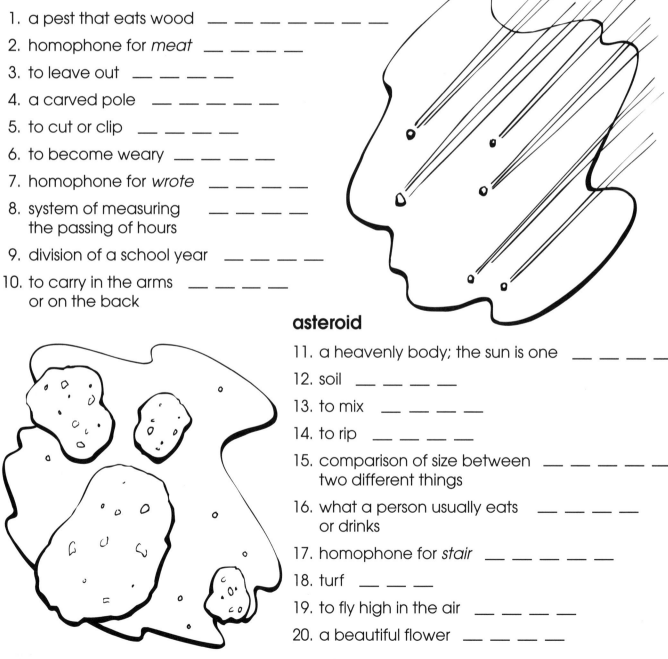

asteroid

11. a heavenly body; the sun is one _ _ _ _ _
12. soil _ _ _ _ _
13. to mix _ _ _ _ _
14. to rip _ _ _ _ _
15. comparison of size between two different things _ _ _ _ _ _
16. what a person usually eats or drinks _ _ _ _ _
17. homophone for *stair* _ _ _ _ _ _
18. turf _ _ _ _
19. to fly high in the air _ _ _ _ _
20. a beautiful flower _ _ _ _ _

National
Geography
Awareness
Week

Name _____

All Around the Globe

National Geography Awareness Week is celebrated during November. It is a great time to appreciate the many fascinating countries, customs, and cultures that make up the world.

Unscramble the words below and on page 24 to spell the names of countries. Write them in the boxes. Then, unscramble the letters in the shaded boxes of each puzzle to find out on (or near) which continents the countries are located.

1. daaanc

2. cimoxe

3. nardaag

4. tiedun ttseas

5. thiia

6. maaacji

7. beezil

8. socat cria

___ ___ ___ ___ ___ ___ ___

___ ___ ___ ___ ___ ___

1. manrusie

2. bamlicoo

3. roadcue

4. nieaantgr

5. liazrb

6. ruep

7. guruyau

8. liech

___ ___ ___ ___ ___ ___ ___

___ ___ ___ ___ ___ ___

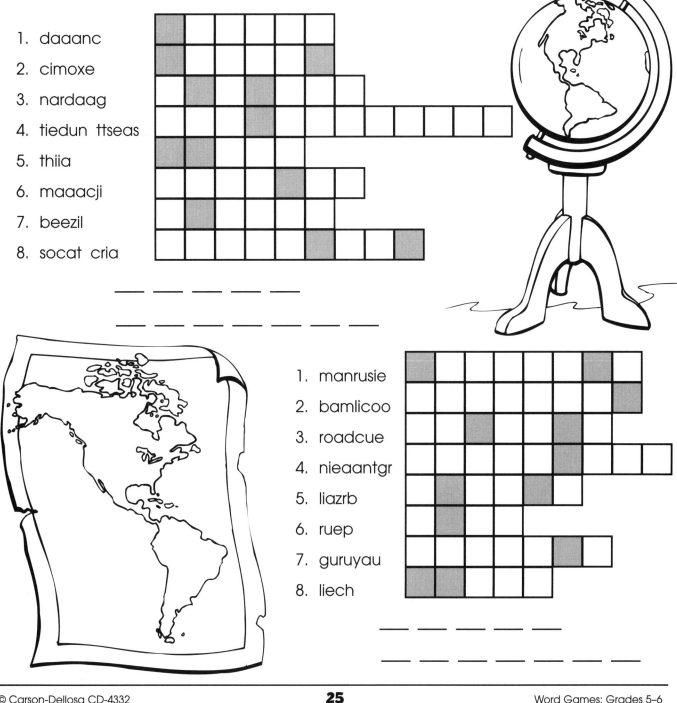

Name _____

All Around the Globe

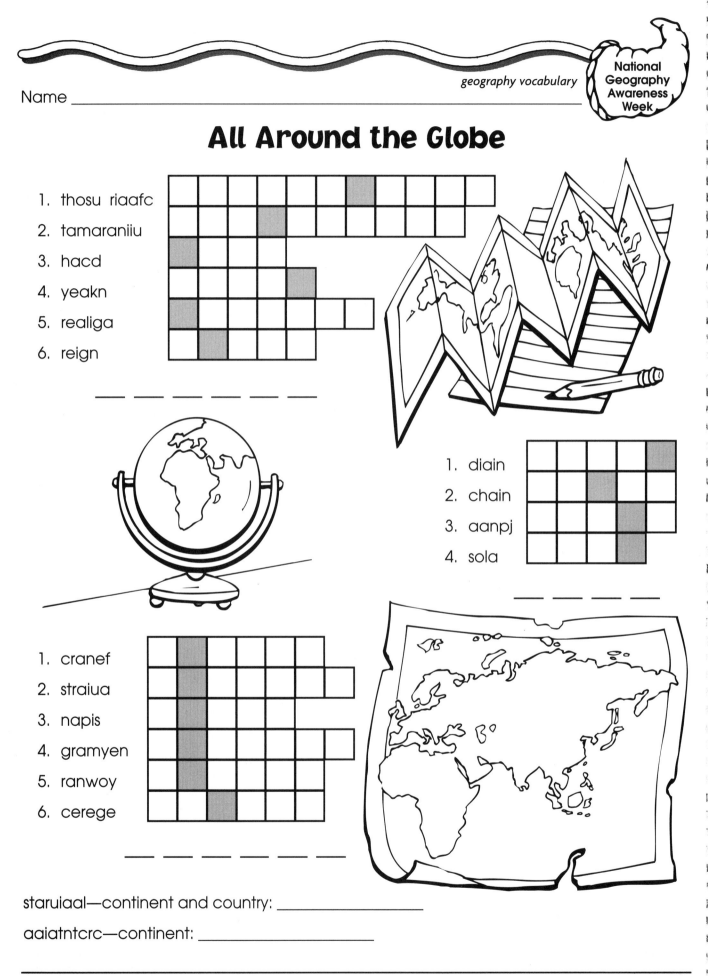

1. thosu riaafc
2. tamaraniiu
3. hacd
4. yeakn
5. realiga
6. reign

_ _ _ _ _ _ _ _ _

1. diain
2. chain
3. aanpj
4. sola

_ _ _ _ _ _

1. cranef
2. straiua
3. napis
4. gramyen
5. ranwoy
6. cerege

_ _ _ _ _ _

staruiaal—continent and country: _____

aaiatntcrc—continent: _____

Name _____

Eat Lightly

An apple a day keeps the doctor away. This popular saying might be heard during November— Good Nutrition Month.

Unscramble the letters to discover twelve words relating to food. Then, use each word to complete the analogies below.

coalhotce   __ ◯◯ __ __ __ __ __

dupgidn   ◯ __ __ __ __ __ __

thetiagps   __ __ __ __ __ ◯ __

grotuy   __ ◯ __ __ __ __

tiicsub   __ __ ◯ __ ◯ __

urags   ◯ __ __ ◯ __

fitur   __ __ __ __ ◯

lepap   __ ◯ __ __ __

realce   __ __ __ __ __ __

felfaw   __ __ __ __ __ __

1. Sour is to lemon as sweet is to _____ .

2. Frosting is to cake as syrup is to _____ .

3. Fiction is to nonfiction as vegetable is to _____ .

4. Fruit is to orange as bread is to _____ .

5. Knead is to need as serial is to _____ .

6. Vine is to grapes as tree is to _____ .

7. Crunchy is to carrots as creamy is to _____ .

8. Vegetable is to corn as candy is to _____ .

9. Grain is to oats as milk is to _____ .

10. Mexican is to burrito as Italian is to _____ .

Unscramble the circled letters above to answer this question:

What popular snack food was invented by George Crumb?

__ __ __ __ __   __ __ __ __ __ __

Name _____

Just Say "no!"

One little two-letter word is very important when it comes to drugs. This word is NO! Say "no" to drugs and "yes" to a healthy body and mind. One day in November is set aside to help people try to quit smoking.

Complete each puzzle using the letter clues and the clues below.

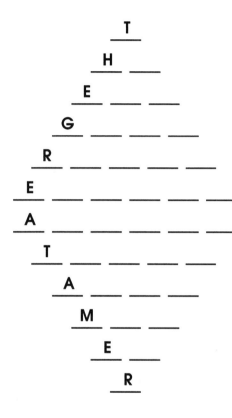

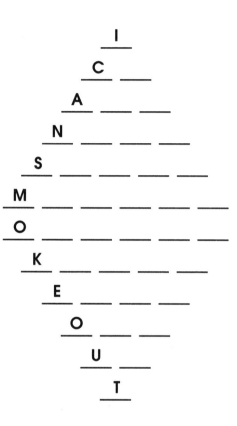

1. first letter of a word for *journey*	1. homophone for *eye*
2. hello	2. letter abbreviation for *carbon dioxide*
3. antonym for *beginning*	3. a deed; something done
4. synonym for *present*	4. midday
5. cowboy competition	5. to take by force
6. sufficient	6. building that houses works of art
7. sounds like *except*	7. to oppose something firmly
8. homophone for *there*	8. light canoe
9. dull, steady pain	9. direction where the sun rises
10. wet dirt	10. antonym for *in*
11. abbreviation for *emergency room*	11. you and me
12. 18th letter of the alphabet	12. 20th letter of the alphabet

Name _____

Let's Give Thanks

Americans give thanks for their many blessings every year on Thanksgiving. It is a day full of food, family, and thankfulness.

Complete the puzzle with words relating to Thanksgiving. The letters that have been provided are part of George Washington's name. This U. S. president proclaimed Thanksgiving Day as the fourth Thursday in November.

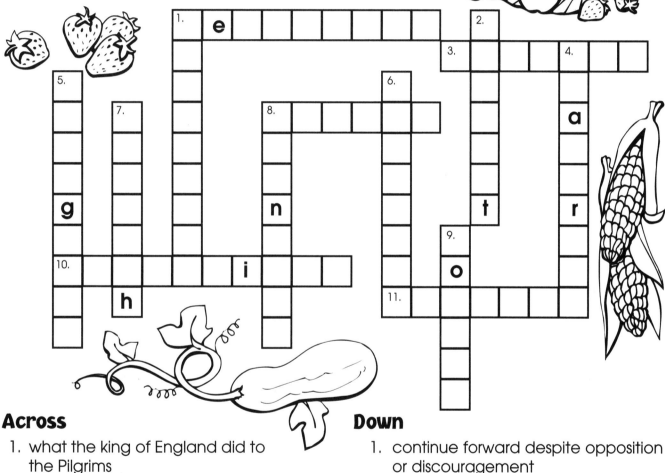

Across

1. what the king of England did to the Pilgrims
3. to gather a crop
8. to be outside of one's own country
10. to be grateful for
11. to remain alive or in existence

Down

1. continue forward despite opposition or discouragement
2. a feast
4. a very *detailed* dinner
5. person who makes a home in a foreign country
6. starving
7. the *victory* of the Pilgrims
8. very plentiful
9. small bit of food

Name _____

Air Fun

November is Aviation History Month. It celebrates the aeronautical experiments of two brothers, Joseph Michel and Jacques Etienne Montgolfier of France.

To find out how they achieved man's first flight in November 1782, use each clue to write a word that begins with the prefix *dis-* or *mis-*. Then, use the number code to complete the box below.

to vanish

‾‾ ‾‾ ‾‾ ‾‾ ‾‾ ‾‾ ‾‾ ‾‾ ‾‾
18 28 27 16 11 13 14 40 34

to spell incorrectly

‾‾ ‾‾ ‾‾ ‾‾ ‾‾ ‾‾ ‾‾ ‾‾
    6   27 55 11 3   8   7

to differ in opinion

‾‾ ‾‾ ‾‾ ‾‾ ‾‾ ‾‾ ‾‾ ‾‾
10 33 55 12 26 38 42 3

to deceive ‾‾ ‾‾ ‾‾ ‾‾ ‾‾ ‾‾ ‾‾
            6   27 20 39 45 10

to break the connection

‾‾ ‾‾ ‾‾ ‾‾ ‾‾ ‾‾ ‾‾ ‾‾ ‾‾ ‾‾
18 46 27 19 21 17 54 9   37 29

to abuse ‾‾ ‾‾ ‾‾ ‾‾ ‾‾ ‾‾ ‾‾
          33 55 31 15 42 49 35

to see or learn about something before anyone else

‾‾ ‾‾ ‾‾ ‾‾ ‾‾ ‾‾ ‾‾ ‾‾
10 6   27 37 52   9   38

to lose something

‾‾ ‾‾ ‾‾ ‾‾ ‾‾ ‾‾ ‾‾
28 55 13 8   40 37 9

to be a liar or a cheater

‾‾ ‾‾ ‾‾ ‾‾ ‾‾ ‾‾ ‾‾ ‾‾ ‾‾
10 46 27 23 53 54 39 27 41

to behave badly

‾‾ ‾‾ ‾‾ ‾‾ ‾‾ ‾‾ ‾‾ ‾‾
    6   55 24 14 2   25   42

not faithful ‾‾ ‾‾ ‾‾ ‾‾ ‾‾ ‾‾ ‾‾ ‾‾
              18 33 27 50 30 4   32 51

a mistake in something printed

‾‾ ‾‾ ‾‾ ‾‾ ‾‾ ‾‾ ‾‾
28 55 11 15 46 17 22

to shame or humiliate

‾‾ ‾‾ ‾‾ ‾‾ ‾‾ ‾‾ ‾‾ ‾‾
18 6   55 26 34 25 19 39

bad luck

‾‾ ‾‾ ‾‾ ‾‾ ‾‾ ‾‾ ‾‾ ‾‾
28 27 5   36 47 1   17 3

to get off a horse

‾‾ ‾‾ ‾‾ ‾‾ ‾‾ ‾‾ ‾‾
18 6   27   43   17 44

to undress ‾‾ ‾‾ ‾‾ ‾‾ ‾‾ ‾‾
            10 6   27 15 30 48

1	2	3	4		5	6	7	8	9	10		11	12	13	14	15		16	17	18
19	20	21	22	23		24	25	26	27		W	28	29	H		H	30	31	
32	33	34		35	36		37	38	39	40	41	42		H	43	44		45	46	47
48	49	50	51	52	53	54	55	.												

Name _____

Follow the Golden Rule

World Kindness Day is in November. What a nice world we would live in if all the world celebrated it! On this day, remember to be kind to others.

Write a word for each clue. Then, use the number code to complete the boxes with words relating to kindness. Two of the words are synonyms, and one is an antonym.

1	2	3	4	5	6	7	8

antonym for *no* ___ ___ ___
8 6 7

place to buy groceries ___ ___ ___ ___ ___
7 5 2 4 6

a long trip for pleasure and sight-seeing ___ ___ ___ ___
5 2 3 4

use a knife to do this ___ ___ ___
1 3 5

1	2	3	4	5	6	7	8	9	10

a sharp end ___ ___ ___ ___ ___
1 2 4 7 5

antonym for *more* ___ ___ ___ ___
3 8 9 10

to ruin ___ ___ ___ ___ ___
9 1 2 4 3

a flight of stairs ___ ___ ___ ___ ___
9 5 6 1 10

1	2	3	4	5	6	7	8

what we call ourselves ___ ___ ___ ___ ___
4 3 1 2 8

a jumble ___ ___ ___ ___
1 6 8 7

antonym for *woman* ___ ___ ___
1 3 5

large, high rock with steep sides and a flat top ___ ___ ___ ___
1 6 8 3

Name _____

Everglade National Park Dedicated

A Perfect Park

On December 6, 1947, President Harry S. Truman dedicated the Everglades National Park in Florida. Encompassing more than one million acres, it is the only place in the world where alligators and crocodiles coexist in nature.

All of the words below relate to one of the biomes listed in the chart. Write each word under the correct biome and cross it off. Then, write the seven remaining words in order to find out what happens when crocodiles keep their mouths open to cool off.

_____ _____ _____ _____

_____ _____ _____ .

Gila monsters	long, dry season	camels	hippos	elm trees
squirrels	birds	giraffes	polar bears	deer
oak trees	extremely cold	pick	palm trees	leftover
food	jaguars	wet	zebra	kangaroos
raccoons	from	frozen subsoil	their	oasis
dry	humid	cacti	elephants	lions
monkeys	penguins	climbing vines	teeth	arctic foxes

Tundra	Desert	Rain Forest	Savanna & Woodland	Temperate Forest

Name _____

Congratulations, Mr. Amundsen

On December 14, 1911, Roald Amundsen, a Norwegian explorer, led the first expedition to reach the South Pole.

Circle each travel-related word from the Word Bank in the puzzle. The words appear horizontally, vertically, and diagonally. Then, write the uncircled letters in order on the blanks to find out what Amundsen had originally hoped to discover.

— —   — —   — — — — —   — —

— — — — —   — —   — — —   — —

— — — — — —   — —   — — — — —

— — — —   — — —   — — — —

— — —   — — — — — — — — — — —

— — — — —   **had just** — — — — — — —   — t .

h	e	w	a	s	r	e	c	r	e	a	t	i	o	n
s	a	b	o	u	i	t	t	t	r	a	v	e	l	e
o	l	e	e	r	e	g	n	e	s	s	a	p	a	g
v	e	g	b	r	o	c	h	u	r	e	e	t	o	d
t	r	a	n	s	p	o	r	t	a	t	i	o	n	o
o	o	g	t	r	y	t	o	d	s	i	s	c	j	l
u	l	g	a	g	e	n	d	a	o	e	v	e	o	u
r	p	a	r	t	h	e	n	o	x	r	e	t	u	g
i	x	b	n	o	i	t	a	c	a	v	h	i	r	g
s	e	p	o	l	e	w	u	h	a	e	n	h	n	a
t	e	c	a	m	e	r	a	l	e	t	a	r	e	g
n	e	d	c	o	s	m	m	a	n	d	l	e	y	e
r	p	s	n	i	a	t	n	u	o	m	e	a	r	r
y	t	r	o	p	s	s	a	p	r	e	a	c	s	h
s	t	n	e	m	e	g	n	a	r	r	a	e	d	i

Word Bank

transportation
camera
lodge
arrangements
agenda
excursion
brochure
vacation
luggage
mountains
travel
baggage
atlas
journey
passenger
passport
sight-seeing
recreation
tourist
explore

Name _____

Good Job, Mr. Wright!

Orville Wright made the first heavier-than-air flight on December 17, 1903. It is said that aviation was born on this day on the sand dunes at Kitty Hawk, North Carolina. What an accomplishment!

Accomplishment ends with the suffix *-ment*. Read the clues to write words ending in *-ment* in the boxes. Then, use the number code to fill in the blanks below to learn something else that happened in December.

1. an understanding

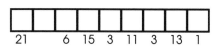

‾21‾ ‾‾ ‾6‾ ‾15‾ ‾3‾ ‾11‾ ‾3‾ ‾13‾ ‾1‾

2. something that charms or delights

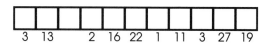

‾3‾ ‾13‾ ‾‾ ‾2‾ ‾16‾ ‾22‾ ‾1‾ ‾11‾ ‾3‾ ‾27‾ ‾19‾

3. area of land built with new homes

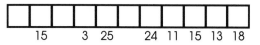

‾‾ ‾15‾ ‾‾ ‾3‾ ‾25‾ ‾‾ ‾24‾ ‾11‾ ‾15‾ ‾13‾ ‾18‾

4. food or drink

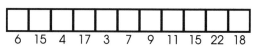

‾6‾ ‾15‾ ‾4‾ ‾17‾ ‾3‾ ‾7‾ ‾9‾ ‾11‾ ‾15‾ ‾22‾ ‾18‾

5. act of making something known

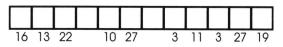

‾16‾ ‾13‾ ‾22‾ ‾‾ ‾10‾ ‾27‾ ‾‾ ‾3‾ ‾11‾ ‾3‾ ‾27‾ ‾19‾

6. colony

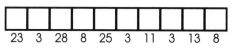

‾23‾ ‾3‾ ‾28‾ ‾8‾ ‾25‾ ‾3‾ ‾11‾ ‾3‾ ‾13‾ ‾8‾

7. something achieved by work or skill

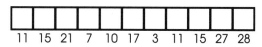

‾21‾ ‾‾ ‾9‾ ‾5‾ ‾3‾ ‾‾ ‾15‾ ‾11‾ ‾15‾ ‾13‾ ‾19‾

8. act of measuring

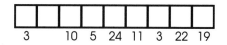

‾11‾ ‾15‾ ‾21‾ ‾7‾ ‾10‾ ‾17‾ ‾3‾ ‾11‾ ‾15‾ ‾27‾ ‾28‾

9. synonym for *achievement*

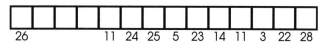

‾26‾ ‾‾ ‾‾ ‾11‾ ‾24‾ ‾25‾ ‾5‾ ‾23‾ ‾14‾ ‾11‾ ‾3‾ ‾22‾ ‾28‾

10. supplies

‾3‾ ‾‾ ‾10‾ ‾5‾ ‾24‾ ‾11‾ ‾3‾ ‾22‾ ‾19‾

11. act of encouraging

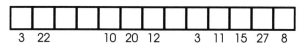

‾3‾ ‾22‾ ‾‾ ‾10‾ ‾20‾ ‾12‾ ‾‾ ‾3‾ ‾11‾ ‾15‾ ‾27‾ ‾8‾

12. lowest floor of a building, partly below ground

‾12‾ ‾7‾ ‾15‾ ‾11‾ ‾15‾ ‾22‾ ‾8‾

‾1‾ ‾2‾ ‾3‾ ‾‾ ‾4‾ ‾5‾ ‾6‾ ‾7‾ ‾8‾ ‾‾ ‾9‾ ‾10‾ ‾11‾ ‾12‾ ‾13‾ ‾‾ ‾14‾ ‾15‾ ‾16‾ ‾17‾ ‾18‾

‾19‾ ‾20‾ ‾21‾ ‾22‾ ‾23‾ ‾24‾ ‾25‾ ‾26‾ ‾27‾ ‾28‾ **was performed by Christian Barnard, a**

South African surgeon, on December 3, 1967.

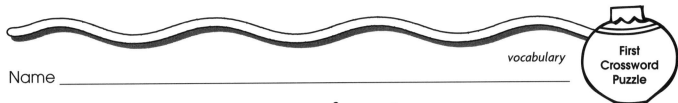

Name _____

A Puzzling Paper

The first crossword puzzle appeared in the *New York World* on December 21, 1913. It was invented by Arthur Wynne.

Use the clues to complete the crossword puzzle with the names of other outstanding inventions or discoveries.

Across

3. underwater ship
5. used to make distant objects seem closer
7. used to take pictures
9. car
11. round with spokes
12. used to make tiny things look larger
13. can fly backward, forward, up, and down

Down

1. used to cook food; flame
2. very tall building
3. sends sound waves through water
4. used for talking to people far away
5. watched every day by millions of people
6. can drill holes in diamonds and perform delicate eye surgery
8. the foundation of modern computers
10. provides power for spacecraft

Happy Hanukkah

Hanukkah, or Festival of Lights, celebrates the restoration of a holy temple in Jerusalem in 165 B.C. It lasts for eight days, beginning on the 25th day of the month of Kislev.

To learn more about Hanukkah, write a word in the boxes for each clue. To help you, each letter has the same number.

1. _____ of Lights

1	2	3	4	5	6	7	8

2. a Jewish toy the Jews pretended to play with when soldiers came near

9	10	2	5	9	2	8

3. the candle used to light the other eight candles in a menorah

3	11	7	12	12	2	3

4. what *Hanukkah* means

9	2	9	5	13	7	4	5	14	15

5. a Jewish religious leader

10	7	16	16	5

6. During Hanukkah, Jewish people are thankful that their religion _____ .

3	17	10	6	5	6	2	9

7. leader of Jewish soldiers

18	17	9	7	3		12	7	13	13	7	16	2	2

8. potato pancakes, eaten during Hanukkah

8	7	4	19	2	3

9. Hanukkah is *an inherited custom.*

4	10	7	9	5	4	5	14	15

10. The dreidel's initials signify "a great _____ occurred there."

12	5	10	7	13	8	2

11. A menorah has this many candles.

15	5	15	2

12. given each night of Hanukkah

20	5	1	4	3

13. a nine-branched candelabrum

12	2	15	14	10	7	11

14. where Jewish people worship

4	2	12	21	8	2

15. The Jews fought against worshipping Greek _____ .

20	14	9	3

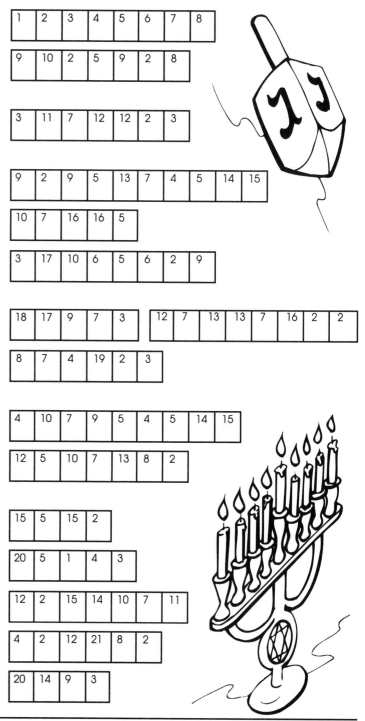

36

Name _____

Merry Christmas

Christmas recognizes the birth of Jesus Christ and involves many special events and traditions.

Use the letters in *Christmas* and the clues to write four-, five-, and six-letter words.

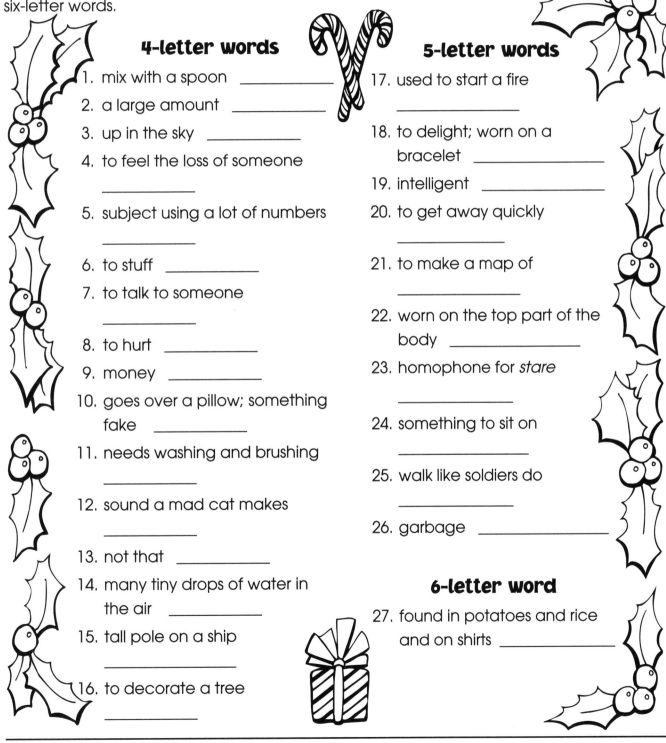

4-letter words

1. mix with a spoon _____

2. a large amount _____

3. up in the sky _____

4. to feel the loss of someone _____

5. subject using a lot of numbers _____

6. to stuff _____

7. to talk to someone _____

8. to hurt _____

9. money _____

10. goes over a pillow; something fake _____

11. needs washing and brushing _____

12. sound a mad cat makes _____

13. not that _____

14. many tiny drops of water in the air _____

15. tall pole on a ship _____

16. to decorate a tree _____

5-letter words

17. used to start a fire _____

18. to delight; worn on a bracelet _____

19. intelligent _____

20. to get away quickly _____

21. to make a map of _____

22. worn on the top part of the body _____

23. homophone for *stare* _____

24. something to sit on _____

25. walk like soldiers do _____

26. garbage _____

6-letter word

27. found in potatoes and rice and on shirts _____

Name _____

Let's Celebrate

Kwanzaa, an African-American celebration, is based on traditional African harvest festivals. It begins December 26 and lasts seven days.

The holiday focuses on *Nguzo Saba*, seven principles of African-American culture. Use the table to translate the Swahili words to English to learn what these principles are.

	K	W	A^1	N	Z	A^2	A^3
1	C	R	X	S	H	U	Q
2	P	Y	A	E	P	J	F
3	O	B	N	K	O	G	L
4	B	N	W	Y	E	F	R
5	L	D	L	T	I	S	J
6	K	A	N	U	T	R	C
7	M	Z	G	V	H	I	M

1. *Umoja* ___ ___ ___ ___ ___
   A^21 A^13 A^27 N5 W2

2. *Kujichagulia* ___ ___ ___ ___-
   N1 N2 K5 A^24

   ___ ___ ___ ___ ___ ___ ___ ___ ___ ___ ___ ___
   W5 Z4 Z6 N2 A^34 K7 Z5 A^16 W6 N5 A^27 K3 W4

3. *Ujima* ___ ___ ___ ___ ___ ___ ___ ___ ___ ___
   K1 Z3 A^15 A^33 N2 A^36 N5 A^27 N7 Z4

   ___ ___ ___ ___ ___ ___ ___
   A^14 Z3 A^34 N3 A^12 A^16 W5

   ___ ___ ___ ___ ___ ___ ___ ___ ___ ___ ___ ___ ___ ___
   W1 Z4 N1 K2 Z3 A^13 A^25 Z5 W3 A^27 A^15 Z5 N5 N4

4. *Ujamaa* ___ ___ ___ ___ ___ ___ ___ ___ ___ ___ ___
   K1 Z3 K3 Z2 N2 A^26 W6 Z6 Z5 N7 Z4

   ___ ___ ___ ___ ___ ___ ___ ___ ___
   N2 K1 K3 W4 Z3 K7 A^27 A^36 N1

5. *Nia* ___ ___ ___ ___ ___ ___ ___
   K2 N6 A^34 Z2 Z3 A^25 N2

6. *Kuumba* ___ ___ ___ ___ ___ ___ ___ ___ ___ ___
   A^36 W1 Z4 A^12 N5 Z5 N7 A^27 Z6 W2

7. *Imani* ___ ___ ___ ___ ___
   A^24 W6 Z5 N5 Z7

During Kwanzaa, a ___ ___ ___ ___ ___ ___ is lit each
K1 A^12 W4 W5 A^15 Z4

night, and the principle of the day is discussed. The

celebration ends with a *karamu*, or ___ ___ ___ ___ ___ ,
A^24 N2 W6 N1 Z6

and an exchange of ___ ___ ___ ___ ___ .
A^23 A^27 A^24 N5 N1

vocabulary   **Card Playing Day**

Just for Fun

Card Playing Day is December 28. What a great time to shuffle cards and play some of your favorite games!

Unscramble the words on each card below to learn about another important event that occurred on December 15, 1791.

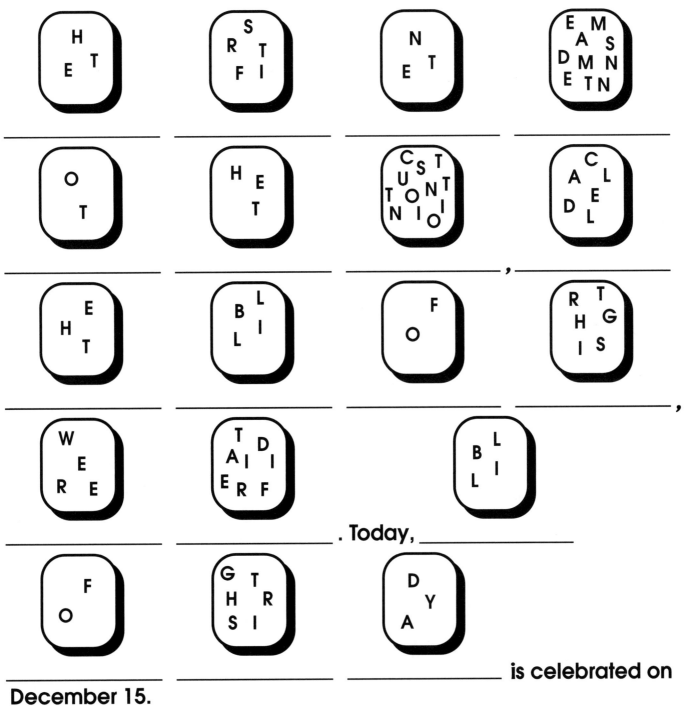

_____ _____ _____ _____

_____ _____ _____ , _____

_____ _____ _____ _____ ,

_____ _____ . Today, _____

_____ _____ _____ is celebrated on

December 15.

Bingo
Created

Bingo

Bingo is a lot of fun for people of all ages. It was created in December 1929.

Use the letters on the Bingo card to complete the list of words. Each group of letters will be used once. Then, unscramble the boxed letters to find out what fun recreational equipment was patented in December 1884.

___ ___ ___ ___ ___ ___ ___   ___ ___ ___ ___ ___

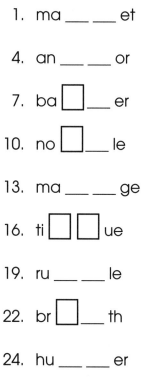

B	I	n	G	O
ng	rd	ea	ha	la
en	ov	rb	mb	ow
ch	ti	gn	wa	ss
le	ui	id	re	na
od	ce	ki	ai	ru

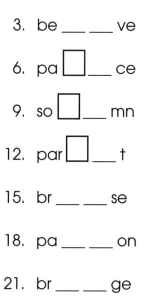

1. ma ___ ___ et

2. cr ___ ___ se

3. be ___ ___ ve

4. an ___ ___ or

5. bi [ ] ___ ng

6. pa [ ] ___ ce

7. ba [ ] ___ er

8. pr ___ ___ se

9. so [ ] ___ mn

10. no [ ] ___ le

11. wr [ ] ___ ch

12. par [ ] ___ t

13. ma ___ ___ ge

14. re ___ ___ nt

15. br ___ ___ se

16. ti [ ][ ] ue

17. lo [ ] ___ on

18. pa ___ ___ on

19. ru ___ ___ le

20. co ___ [ ] rd

21. br ___ ___ ge

22. br [ ] ___ th

23. st ___ ___ ck

24. hu ___ ___ er

25. cl ___ ___ er

Name _____

Sitting Down for What's Right

Do you know who is often credited with starting the civil rights movement? This person refused to give up her seat on a bus in December 1955.

To find out, read each clue and write the answer in the boxes. Each answer will go one letter past the next number. This is because each new word begins with the last two letters of the word before it. Then, write the shaded letters in order on the blanks.

___ ___ ___ ___   ___ ___ k ___

1. the figure formed by two straight lines meeting at a point

2. material made from animal skin; used to make coats, belts, and shoes

3. to wear away

4. periods of 10 years

5. to get free

6. lasting forever

7. synonym for *though*

8. a shadowy trace

9. something that has been built

10. to set free

11. not connected to something else

12. a fellow member of a team

13. a game in which a racket is used

14. homophone for *aisle*

15. a major part of many salads

16. a small, worm-like animal

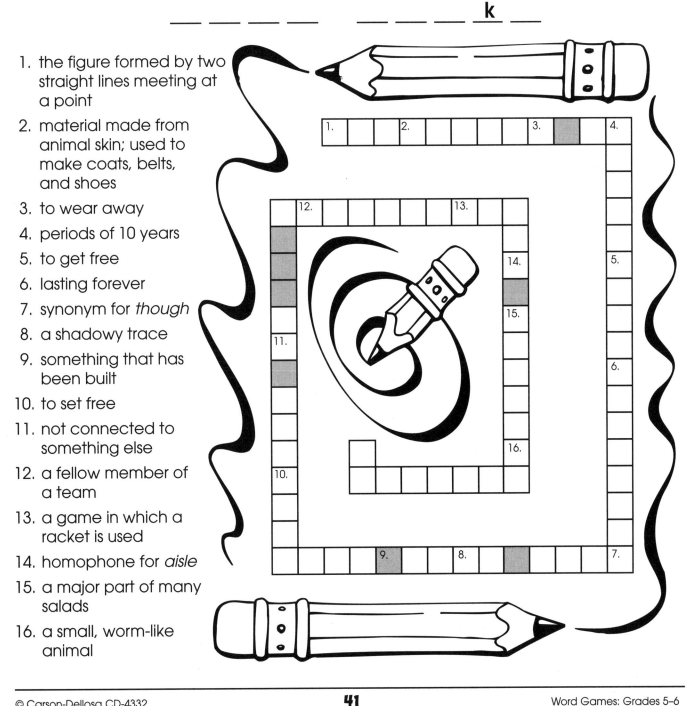

A New Beginning

January is the first month on the Gregorian calendar. The name comes from *Januarius*, a Latin word relating to the Roman god Janus.

The word *January* contains two *a*'s. Each puzzle begins with the letter *a*. Read the clues. Add one letter to each word up to the fifth clue. Then, remove one letter from each word until only *a* is left. The letters can be in any order.

a

— — 1. on, in, near, or by

— — — 2. past tense of *sit*

— — — — 3. a 5-pointed shape

— — — — — 4. begin

— — — — 5. antonym for *sweet*

— — — 6. black and sticky

— — 7. Hoo __ __ y!

a

a

— — 1. abbreviation for *teacher's assistant*

— — — 2. used to hit a ball

— — — — 3. to pound

— — — — — 4. a monster

— — — — 5. where you can sit

— — — 6. to chew food and swallow

— — 7. two vowels that make the long $\bar{e}$ sound

a

a

— — 1. equally

— — — 2. form of verb *have*

— — — — 3. money

— — — — — 4. loud, smashing noise

— — — — 5. skin irritation

— — — 6. what a cheerleader says

— — 7. a sound made to show pain or delight

a

a

— — 1. first two letters of the alphabet

— — — 2. taxi

— — — — 3. flat shellfish with claws

— — — — — 4. to make ready for a jolt

— — — — 5. a contest

— — — 6. automobile

— — 7. abbreviation for California

a

Alaska
Becomes
a State

Name _____

State the States

Alaska became the 49th state on January 3, 1959. Write the state for each state capital in the puzzle.

Across

1. Indianapolis
5. Montgomery
7. Albany
10. Lincoln
13. Austin
14. Atlanta
15. Sacramento
17. Springfield
18. Carson City

Down

1. Boise
2. Tallahassee
3. Olympia
4. Augusta
6. Little Rock
8. Frankfort
9. Charleston
11. Salt Lake City
12. Columbus
16. Des Moines

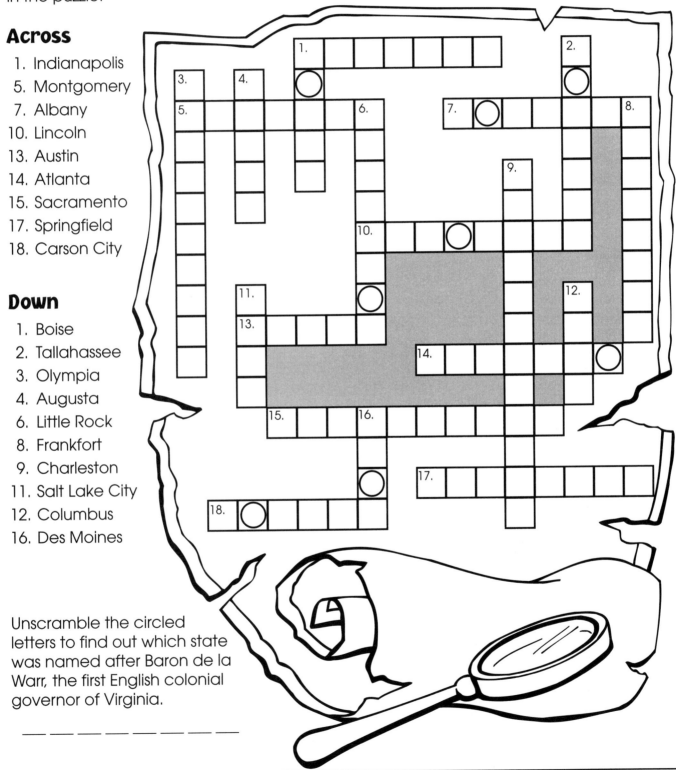

Unscramble the circled letters to find out which state was named after Baron de la Warr, the first English colonial governor of Virginia.

___ ___ ___ ___ ___ ___ ___ ___

43

Name _____

Universal Letter-Writing Week

Nothing Better Than a Letter

Universal Letter-Writing Week is held the beginning of January. It is the perfect time to write a letter or send an E-mail to grandparents, cousins, and friends. However, do not forget to use good grammar! Circle the grammar word from the Word Bank in the puzzle. The words appear horizontally, vertically, and diagonally.

Word Bank

conjunction	English	subject	predicate
quotation mark	verb	hyphen	syllable
proper noun	comma	vowel	contraction
punctuation	adverb	pronoun	period
sentence	clause	article	consonant
adjective	essay	phrase	preposition

```
q  p  r  o  p  e  r  n  o  u  n  g  o  l  n
d  u  c  o  n  j  u  n  c  t  i  o  n  w  u
a  n  o  p  r  e  p  o  s  i  t  i  o  n  o
e  c  n  t  s  h  s  i  l  g  n  e  h  a  n
v  t  t  v  a  s  u  b  j  e  c  t  y  d  o
i  u  r  d  e  t  a  c  i  d  e  r  p  v  r
t  a  a  i  s  r  i  c  c  o  s  v  h  e  p
c  t  c  w  e  r  b  o  e  d  s  o  e  r  h
e  i  t  e  i  n  m  c  n  a  a  w  n  b  r
j  o  i  l  x  m  l  i  f  m  y  e  o  r  a
d  n  o  c  a  n  i  e  l  b  a  l  l  y  s
a  a  n  i  o  d  o  i  r  e  p  r  n  w  e
n  o  i  t  c  r  s  n  t  o  c  b  k  r  r
d  o  b  r  w  n  c  e  c  n  e  t  n  e  s
e  s  u  a  l  c  c  o  n  s  o  n  a  n  t
```

44

double letters

Beginning of Transatlantic Telephone Service

Name _____

Calling Across the Sea

Before January 7, 1927, communication across the ocean was limited for the most part to letters. On this day, transatlantic commercial telephone service began.

To learn what else was put into commercial service in January 1976, use the clues to write words that have double letters. Then, use the number code to fill in the blanks.

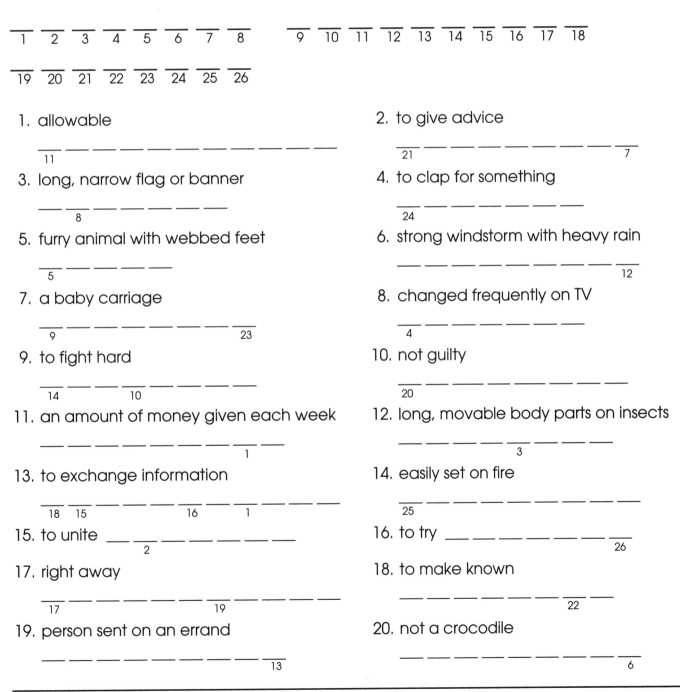

$\overline{\quad}$ $\overline{\quad}$ $\overline{\quad}$ $\overline{\quad}$ $\overline{\quad}$ $\overline{\quad}$ $\overline{\quad}$ $\overline{\quad}$ $\overline{\quad}$ $\overline{\quad}$ $\overline{\quad}$ $\overline{\quad}$ $\overline{\quad}$ $\overline{\quad}$ $\overline{\quad}$ $\overline{\quad}$ $\overline{\quad}$ $\overline{\quad}$
1 2 3 4 5 6 7 8   9 10 11 12 13 14 15 16 17 18

$\overline{\quad}$ $\overline{\quad}$ $\overline{\quad}$ $\overline{\quad}$ $\overline{\quad}$ $\overline{\quad}$ $\overline{\quad}$ $\overline{\quad}$
19 20 21 22 23 24 25 26

1. allowable

   —— — — — — — — — —
   11

2. to give advice

   —— — — — — — — ——
   21   7

3. long, narrow flag or banner

   — — —— — — — —
       8

4. to clap for something

   — —— — — — — —
     24

5. furry animal with webbed feet

   —— — — — —
   5

6. strong windstorm with heavy rain

   — — — — — — — — ——
                    12

7. a baby carriage

   —— — — — — — ——
   9   23

8. changed frequently on TV

   —— — — — — —
   4

9. to fight hard

   —— — —— — — — —
   14   10

10. not guilty

   —— — — — — — —
   20

11. an amount of money given each week

   — — — — — — — —— —
                   1

12. long, movable body parts on insects

   — — — — — —— — —
              3

13. to exchange information

   —— —— — — —— — —— —
   18 15   16   1

14. easily set on fire

   —— — — — — — — —
   25

15. to unite —— —— — — — ——
          2

16. to try —— — — — — — ——
                26

17. right away

   —— — — — — —— — —
   17   19

18. to make known

   — — — — — — —— —
              22

19. person sent on an errand

   — — — — — — — ——
              13

20. not a crocodile

   — — — — — — — ——
              6

Word Games: Grades 5–6

A January Jewel

Benjamin Franklin was an incredible man. Among his many other accomplishments, Franklin proved that lightning was electricity, signed four of the most important documents in U.S. history, and helped establish Pennsylvania's first public hospital and university. He was born on January 17, 1706.

Franklin is to electricity as Edison is to electric light is an analogy. Unscramble the words to complete each analogy below. (Hint: The analogies provide good clues for the scrambled words.)

acmhmttaise	ecibrpnalu	draip	duqeapurlt
_____	_____	_____	_____
pomohas	cadhehae	sreuerpoh	trnosaibtcu
_____	_____	_____	_____
rentcuy	draguteh	rathou	hivesr
_____	_____	_____	_____

1. Bill Clinton is to democrat as George W. Bush is to _____ .

2. Three is to triplet as four is to _____ .

3. Pronouns are to English as fractions are to _____ .

4. Rich is to penniless as slow is to _____ .

5. Johnny Appleseed is to legend as Batman is to _____ .

6. Hands is to soap as hair is to _____ .

7. Division is to multiplication as addition is to _____ .

8. Dad is to Mom as son is to _____ .

9. Song is to songwriter as book is to _____ .

10. Ten is to decade as one hundred is to _____ .

11. Hot is to sweat as cold is to _____ .

12. Stomach is to stomachache as head is to _____ .

First
Thesaurus
Published

Name _____

They Are All the Same

The first thesaurus was published on January 18, 1852. Peter Mark Roget put together a book containing 35,000 synonyms. Write a synonym for each word.

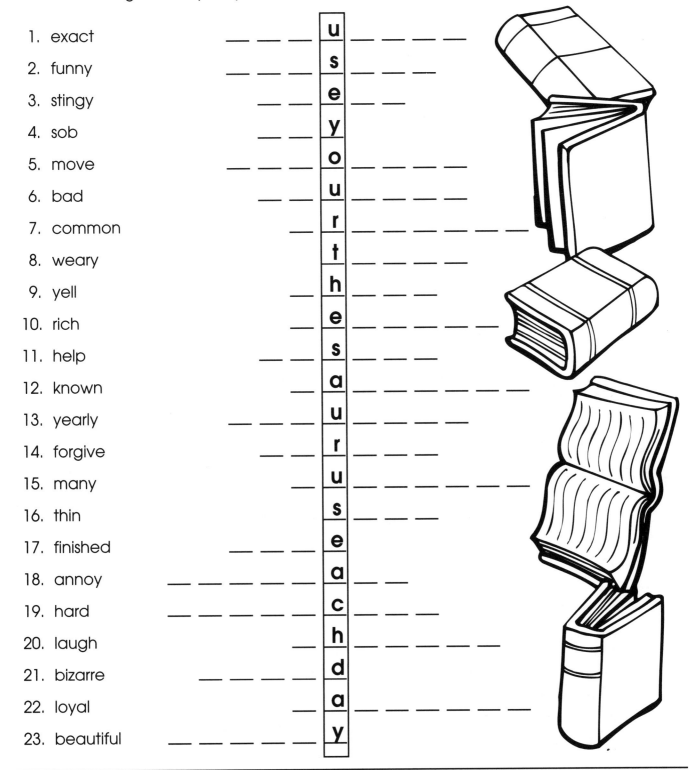

1. exact _ _ _ **u** _ _ _ _ _
2. funny _ _ **s** _ _ _ _
3. stingy _ _ **e** _ _ _
4. sob _ _ **y**
5. move _ _ _ **o** _ _
6. bad _ _ **u** _
7. common _ **r** _ _ _ _ _ _
8. weary _ **t** _ _ _
9. yell _ **h** _ _ _
10. rich _ **e** _ _ _ _ _
11. help _ _ **s** _ _ _
12. known _ _ **a** _ _ _ _
13. yearly _ _ _ **u** _ _ _
14. forgive _ _ **r** _ _ _
15. many _ _ **u** _ _ _ _
16. thin _ _ **s** _ _ _
17. finished _ _ _ **e** _ _
18. annoy _ _ _ _ _ **a** _ _
19. hard _ _ _ _ **c** _ _ _
20. laugh _ _ **h** _ _ _ _ _
21. bizarre _ _ _ **d**
22. loyal _ _ **a** _ _ _ _ _
23. beautiful _ _ _ _ _ **y**

Name _____

Magnificent Men

The third Monday in January is set aside each year to honor Dr. Martin Luther King, Jr. This civil rights leader worked tirelessly to help African-Americans achieve equal rights in the United States.

There is another special day in January that occurs every four years. This event takes place on January 20. To find out what this day is, read the clues and write the answers in the puzzle. When the puzzle is complete, write the outside letter of each word in numerical order on the blanks.

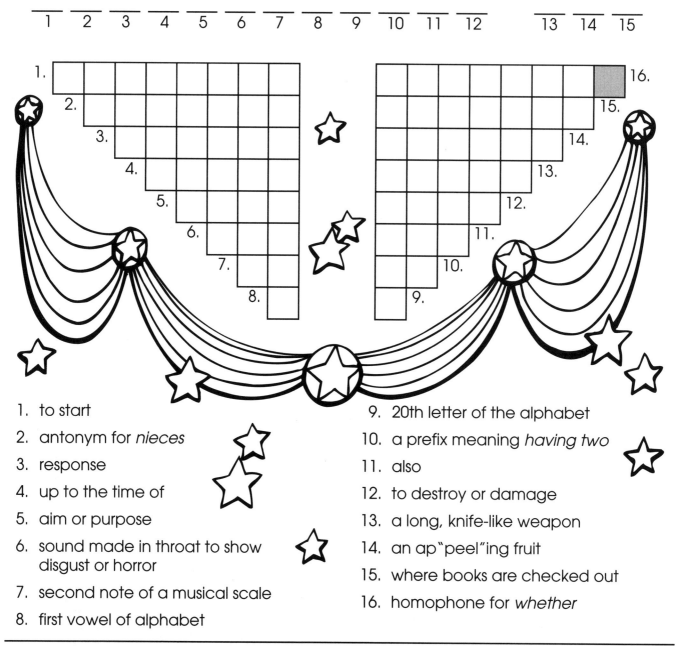

1. to start
2. antonym for *nieces*
3. response
4. up to the time of
5. aim or purpose
6. sound made in throat to show disgust or horror
7. second note of a musical scale
8. first vowel of alphabet

9. 20th letter of the alphabet
10. a prefix meaning *having two*
11. also
12. to destroy or damage
13. a long, knife-like weapon
14. an ap"peel"ing fruit
15. where books are checked out
16. homophone for *whether*

Louis Braille's Birthday

Bravo, Louis Braille!

Louis Braille was born in France in January 1809. At age 15, Braille, who was blind, developed a raised dot-dash system to help blind people read.

Braille contains the long $\bar{a}$ sound. *Blind* contains the long $\bar{i}$ sound. Using the clues, write words containing long $\bar{a}$ (left puzzle) or long $\bar{i}$ (right puzzle) sounds in the boxes. Then, write the letters from the shaded boxes to answer each question below.

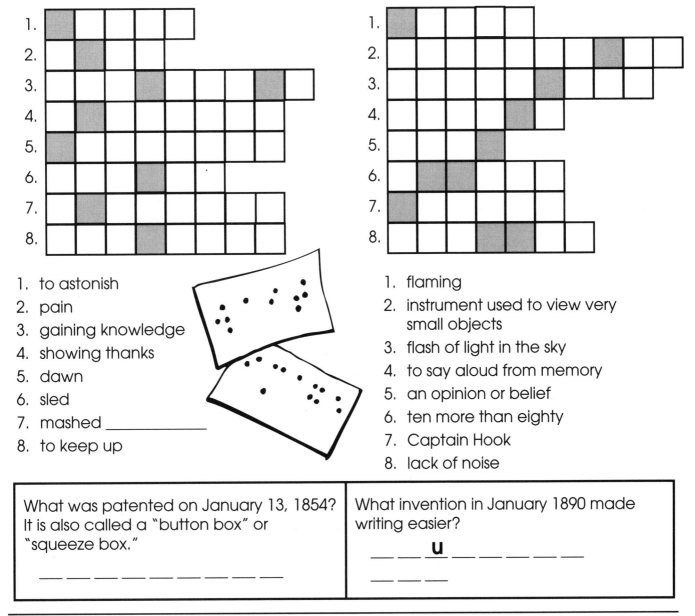

1. to astonish
2. pain
3. gaining knowledge
4. showing thanks
5. dawn
6. sled
7. mashed _____
8. to keep up

1. flaming
2. instrument used to view very small objects
3. flash of light in the sky
4. to say aloud from memory
5. an opinion or belief
6. ten more than eighty
7. Captain Hook
8. lack of noise

What was patented on January 13, 1854? It is also called a "button box" or "squeeze box."	What invention in January 1890 made writing easier?
__ __ __ __ __ __ __ __ __	__ __ **u** __ __ __ __ __

Name _____

Let There Be Light

On December 21, 1879, the world learned about Thomas Edison's fabulous invention— the electric light! Edison was granted the first patent for this incandescent light on January 27, 1880.

Edison's invention of the electric light earned him a famous nickname, based on the location of his laboratory at the time. To find out his nickname, complete each word in the lightbulbs. Then, use the number code to fill in the blanks below. Be careful! More than one letter can complete some words.

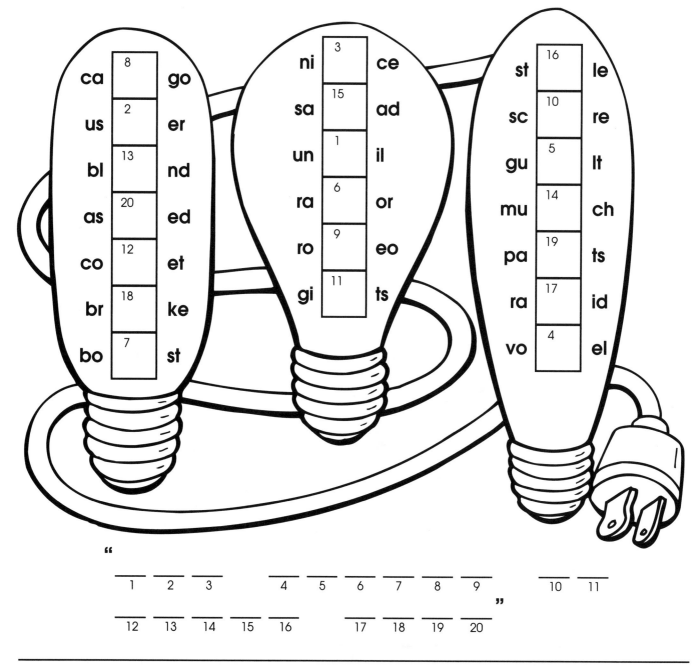

"__ __ __   __ __ __ __ __ __   __ __
  1 2 3   4 5 6 7 8 9   10 11

__ __ __ __ __   __ __ __ __ "
12 13 14 15 16   17 18 19 20

Name _____

Value Your Vision

January is National Eye Care Month. Do not forget to take good care of your eyes. Think of everything you do with them!

The word *pupil* has more than one meaning. For example, *pupil* can be *a student* or *an opening in the center of the eye.*

Write the word for each pair of definitions. Then, write the shaded letters in order on the blanks to complete the sentence below.

1. not absent/a gift
2. strict/back end of a boat
3. to protest/something that can be touched
4. complete/to express with the voice
5. to close tightly/a sea animal
6. a fellow/to become rough
7. a baseball player/a mixture of eggs, flour, and milk
8. go well together/used to start a fire
9. to crowd or squeeze/a game played in a court
10. thin/to stand at a slant
11. tiny/60 seconds
12. land/to keep from flying
13. to abandon/dry, sandy region
14. feeling nervous/verb form
15. firm and steady/where horses live

1.
2.
3.
4.
5.
6.
7.
8.
9.
10.
11.
12.
13.
14.
15.

Hollywood film stars first wore sunglasses, not to look cool, but to __ __ __ __ __ __ __

__ __ __ __ __ __   __ y __ __   from the bright lights.

An Incredible Court

On February 2, 1790, the Supreme Court of the United States met for the first time. The Supreme Court is the highest court in the nation.

Supreme is a word that describes excellence. It means *highest in power, rank, quality, degree, or authority.* Circle the words from the Word Bank in the puzzle. These words all have similar meanings. The words appear horizontally, vertically, and diagonally.

Word Bank

great
magnificent
miraculous
outstanding
awesome
brilliant
spectacular
flawless
incredible
dazzling
perfect
remarkable
wonderful
finest
exceptional
fantastic
ideal
valuable
marvelous
excellent

e	t	n	e	d	i	s	e	f	r	p	p	d	r	o
e	x	t	n	l	a	e	d	i	i	e	i	t	a	u
o	p	c	p	a	a	e	r	n	a	r	n	n	l	t
s	e	c	e	i	w	t	s	e	u	f	c	e	u	s
s	t	j	s	p	n	e	o	s	i	e	r	l	c	t
u	n	f	a	n	t	a	s	t	i	c	e	l	a	a
o	a	v	t	a	c	i	i	o	f	t	d	e	t	n
l	i	a	i	l	a	u	o	q	m	o	i	c	c	d
e	l	l	n	s	t	e	s	n	n	e	b	x	e	i
v	l	u	r	e	m	a	r	k	a	b	l	e	p	n
r	i	a	o	i	t	f	l	a	w	l	e	s	s	g
a	r	b	u	g	n	i	l	z	z	a	d	t	i	t
m	b	l	s	n	s	u	o	l	u	c	a	r	i	m
g	r	e	a	t	l	u	f	r	e	d	n	o	w	o
c	m	a	g	n	i	f	i	c	e	n	t	e	h	t

Starting at the bottom right corner of the puzzle, write the uncircled letters in order to learn the qualifications for becoming a Supreme Court justice.

___ ___ ___   ___ ___ ___ ___ ___ ___ ___ ___ ___ ___   ___ ___ ___

___ ___   ___ ___ ___ ___ ___ ___ ___ ___ ___ ___ ___ ___ ___ ___ .

___ ___ ___ ___ ___ ___ ___ ___   ___ ___ ___

___ ___ ___ ___ ___ ___ ___ ___   **by the**   ___ ___ ___ ___ ___ ___ ___ ___ ___ .

Name _____

Double Trouble

George Herman "Babe" Ruth was born on February 6, 1895. He was the first great home-run hitter in baseball history.

Baseball is a compound word. Use the picture clues to write each compound word.

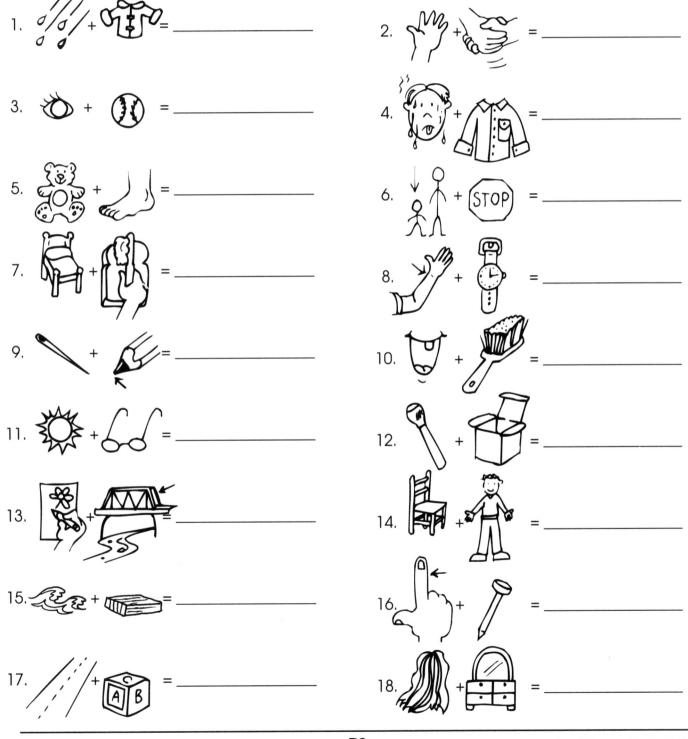

1. _____ + _____ = _____

2. _____ + _____ = _____

3. _____ + _____ = _____

4. _____ + _____ = _____

5. _____ + _____ = _____

6. _____ + _____ = _____

7. _____ + _____ = _____

8. _____ + _____ = _____

9. _____ + _____ = _____

10. _____ + _____ = _____

11. _____ + _____ = _____

12. _____ + _____ = _____

13. _____ + _____ = _____

14. _____ + _____ = _____

15. _____ + _____ = _____

16. _____ + _____ = _____

17. _____ + _____ = _____

18. _____ + _____ = _____

Word Games: Grades 5–6

Name _____

Creative Cooper

Peter Cooper was a noted inventor, manufacturer, and philanthropist. Born on February 12, 1791, Cooper built the famous locomotive, the *Tom Thumb*, the first steam locomotive to operate commercially in America.

Philanthropist contains the digraph *ph*. Sometimes words with *ph* and *gh* are easily misspelled. Use the clues to write words containing *gh* or *ph* in the blanks. The letters in the box will spell the name of the only U.S. president to receive a patent.

1. a person's signature

2. contains 26 letters

3. what pigs eat from

4. a section of a piece of writing

5. picture made with a camera

6. dark, sticky, tar-like substance used to pave roads

7. a victory

8. ha, ha, ha

9. looks like a porpoise

10. antonym for *niece*

11. place to buy medicine

11. not smooth

13. huge animal with a long trunk

14. sufficient

Name _____

Many Terrific Leaders

Presidents' Day is the third Monday in February. It is a day to honor our nation's presidents, especially George Washington and Abraham Lincoln, whose birthdays are February 22 and February 12, respectively.

Read the information about some of the presidents. Then, choose from the presidents listed to answer each clue.

George W. Bush	Andrew Johnson	James Buchanan
Franklin D. Roosevelt	James Monroe	Grover Cleveland
John Tyler	William H. Harrison	James A. Garfield

1. He died on the 4th of July, like John Adams and Thomas Jefferson.

   — — — — —   — — ◯ — —

2. He held office the longest; he was elected four times.

   — — — — — — — — —. — — — — ◯ — — —

3. He served the shortest time in office: one month.

   — — — — — — — —. — — — — — ◯ — — —

4. He had the most children of any president—15! — — — — ◯ — — — —

5. He was the only president who never married.

   — — ◯ — —   — — — — — — — —

6. He never attended school. — — — — — —   ◯ — — — —

7. The "Baby Ruth" candy bar was named in honor of his new daughter, Ruth.

   — — — ◯ —   — — — — — — — — —

8. He was the first left-handed president.

   — — — — — —. — — — — — ◯ — —

9. He is the second president to be the son of a president.

   — — — — — —. — — ◯ — —

Unscramble the circled letters to determine which president died on the 50th anniversary of the Declaration of Independence.

T. — — — — — — — — — —

Name _____

vocabulary

African-American History Month

Great Contributors

February is devoted to honoring the contributions of African-Americans to our country.

To learn about a few of these talented men and women, write the last name of the African-American that each clue describes. Then, use the number code to discover the category that each person belongs to.

| 1 | t | 2 | 3 | 4 | 5 | 4 | 6 |

1. last name of the sisters who won the Sydney, Australia, 2000 Olympics gold medal for women's doubles in tennis.

___ ___ ___ ___ ___ ___ ___
      3 3   6

2. the first African-American professional baseball player

___ ___ ___ ___ ___ ___ ___
           6

3. the first African-American tennis player to win Wimbledon

___ ___ ___ ___
 1 6 2 4

| c | 1 | v | 1 | 2 | | 3 | 1 | g | 4 | t | 5 | | 2 | e | 6 | 7 | e | 8 | 5 |

4. main leader of the U.S. civil rights movement in the 1950s and 1960s

___ ___ ___ ___
   1

5. refused to give up her seat on a bus

___ ___ ___ ___ ___
   6 8   5

6. organized and lead a union for Pullman car porters; helped organize the march in Washington, D.C. in 1963

___ ___ ___ ___ ___ ___
 3 6   7   2   4

| 1 | 2 | 3 | 4 | t | 4 | 5 | 6 | 7 | | f | 4 | g | u | 8 | 9 | 10 |

7. first African-American man to become chairman for the Joint Chiefs of Staff

___ ___ ___ ___ ___ ___
 1 2   9 7 7

8. first African-American woman to serve in U.S. Congress

___ ___ ___ ___ ___ ___
 5   4 10   2 3

9. first African-American woman from a southern state to serve in U.S. Congress; first African-American keynote speaker at a national convention of Democrats

___ ___ ___ ___ ___
  2 8   6

Name _____

Be Kind to Yourself

February is National Boost Self-Esteem Month. Think about all of your good qualities. Maybe you are a great soccer player, a fast reader, a good memorizer, or an energetic volunteer at a nursing home. Whatever you do well, pat yourself on the back for it today. Pat someone else on the back for a job well done, too.

Write the answer to each clue in the puzzle. Then, write the outside letter of each line in order on the blanks to finish the message.

To help build self-esteem,

_ _ _ _ _ _ _ _ _

_ _ _ _ _ _ !

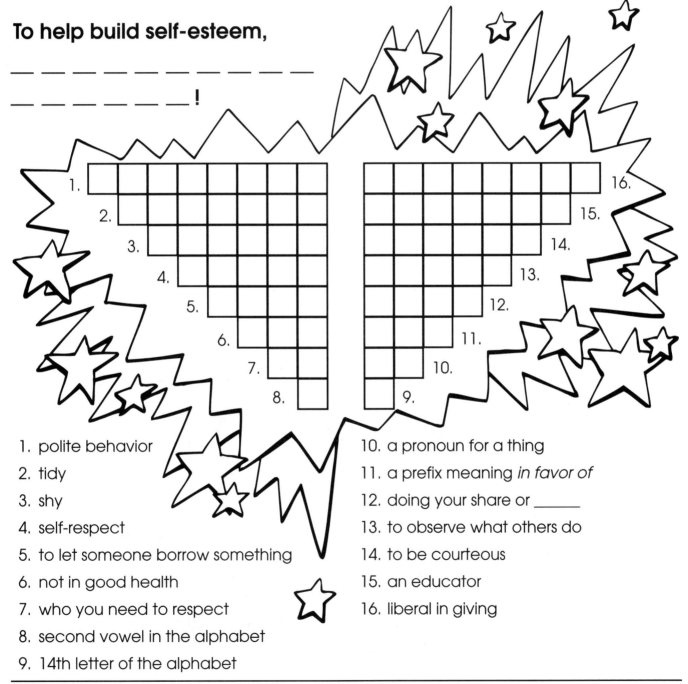

1. polite behavior
2. tidy
3. shy
4. self-respect
5. to let someone borrow something
6. not in good health
7. who you need to respect
8. second vowel in the alphabet
9. 14th letter of the alphabet

10. a pronoun for a thing
11. a prefix meaning *in favor of*
12. doing your share or _____
13. to observe what others do
14. to be courteous
15. an educator
16. liberal in giving

Name _____

Susan B. Anthony's Birthday

What a Woman!

One of the first leaders of the campaign for women's rights was Susan B. Anthony. She helped organize the women's suffrage movement. Anthony was born February 15, 1820.

Campaign contains the silent letter *g*. Words with silent letters are often difficult to spell. Read each phonetic spelling and write the word in the boxes. Each word includes a silent letter. Then, write the shaded letters in order on the blanks to learn another fact about this remarkable woman.

She became the first woman whose picture appeared on a __.__. ____ ____ ____ ____

in ___ ___ ___ ___ ___ ___ ___   ___ ___ ___ ___ ___ ___ ___ ___ ___ ___ ___.

'daủt

'ī(ə)l

'kä-ləm

kən-'dem

'rin-kəl

'nȯ

'fȯr-ən

'sä-ləm

'nōn

'det

'rench

'ī-lənd

'yōk

'rek

'li-sᵊh

'rīm

(ˌ)kam-'pān

'ȯ-təm

'fōk

'när(-ə)ld

'ri-<u>th</u>əm

'rist

'sōrd

'nat

Name _____

Astronomical Men

Nicolaus Copernicus is considered the founder of present-day astronomy. This Polish astronomer developed the theory that the Earth is a moving planet. Copernicus was born on February 19, 1473.

Work your way around the Earth below. Read the clues and write the answers in the boxes. Each answer will go one letter past the next number. This is because each word begins with the last two letters of the word before it. Then, starting with the *g,* write the circled letters in order. This will spell the name of another famous astronomer born on February 15, 1564.

___ ___ ___ ___ ___ ___ ___

1. the planet we live on
2. a subject or topic
3. of moderate or low quality
4. a shape with four right angles
5. *free* time

6. an arrangement for setting something aside, such as a plane ticket
7. one time
8. homophone for *serial*
9. a book published each year with a calendar, weather forecasts, and other information

10. to complete successfully
11. a place that protects someone from weather or danger
12. to wear away
13. synonym for yummy
14. the way of using something

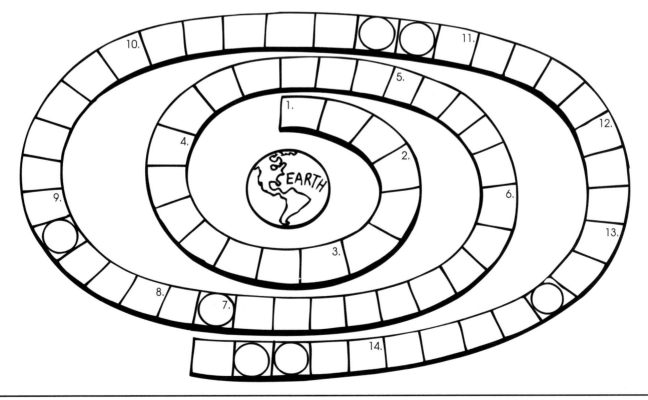

An Awesome Organization

Robert Baden-Powell was born on February 22, 1857. He is the founder of the Boy Scouts of America. This organization teaches boys to be good citizens and trains them to become leaders. It was incorporated on February 8, 1910. Boy Scouts must promise to follow the twelve points in the Scout Law. These points are the qualities a scout strives to have.

Write the answer to each clue in the puzzle. Then, use the number code to complete the Boy Scout motto and teaching method used.

reliable: [ ][7][ ][ ][ ][ ][20][13][ ][ ][18]

faithful to one's country, family, duty, or beliefs: [10][20][18][12][10]

useful: [ ][5][10][3][ ][ ][10]

not hostile: [ ][4][15][8][22][9][10][18]

polite: [ ][20][ ][7][ ][2][20][ ][ ]

nice: [ ][21][16][19]

following orders: [20][1][2][9][15][8][14]

joyful: [ ][ ][11][2][13][ ][ ][10]

showing careful use of money: [ ][ ][4][21][ ][ ][18][ ]

courageous: [17][13][6][ ][ ][5]

not dirty: [ ][10][11][12][16]

respectful: [4][2][ ][11][7][ ][5][14][ ]

___ ___   ___ ___ ___ ___ ___ ___ ___
1   2   3   4   5   3   6   7   8   9

___ ___ ___ ___ ___ ___ ___ g
10 11 12 13 14 15 16

___ ___
17 18

___ ___ ___ ___ g
19 20 21 22

American Heart Month

Name _____

Be Heart Smart

American Heart Month is celebrated in February. It was created to help us realize the importance of keeping our hearts healthy.

To complete the puzzle, use the clues to unscramble each word related to the heart.

Across

3. what the heart is made of (lemcus)
6. make up largest part of heart (centsilver)
7. what the heart pushes blood through (sleevss)
8. used to listen to the heart (thosstceope)
10. the surgical procedure where a person gets a new heart (snaptartln)
12. opposite of *minor* surgery
15. what a person is called while being cared for in a hospital (tentiap)
16. surgery done to unclog arteries (spaysb)

Down

1. carry blood away from heart (trsiraee)
2. high blood pressure; a cause of heart disease (repnehtoynis)
4. relating to the heart and blood vessels (advilcrosaaruc)
5. an *illness* of the heart (seadesi)
9. what 1.25 million Americans suffer from each year; a heart _____ (catkat)
11. a habit that is bad for your heart (kinsgom)
13. what plays a role in heart attacks (tide)
14. form smaller part of heart (arita)

Name _____

Magnificent March

March was named after the Roman god Mars. He was known as both the god of war and the god of vegetation. His name means *boisterous.*

Vegetation ends with the suffix *-ion,* meaning *the act of, the state of being,* or *the result of.* Using the clues, write words ending in *-ion* in each puzzle. Then, write the letters from the shaded boxes in order to spell the names of three U.S. presidents born in March.

1. an advance in rank, level, or position
2. a profession, business, or trade
3. north, south, east, or west
4. talking about something in depth
5. the result of deciding
6. something a person owns
7. to extend the length of time

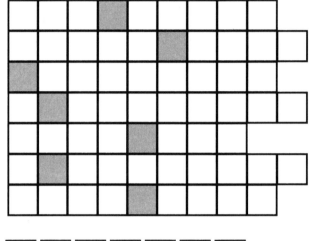

J. __ __ __ __ __ __ __

1. handing down of customs and beliefs
2. member of the same family
3. something suggested
4. the act of interrupting

J. __ __ y __ __ __ __

1. being satisfied
2. act of teaching
3. permission to enter
4. act of working together
5. statement that tells what something means

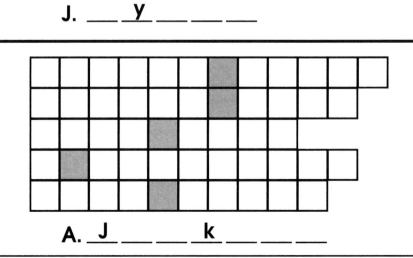

A. J __ __ __ k __ __ __

Read Across America Day

Read, Everyone!

Read Across America Day honors a very famous author of many silly and fun children's books. It takes place on this author's birthday, March 2.

To find out who this famous writer is, read the clues and write the answers on the blanks on each puzzle. Then, beginning with the puzzle on the left, write the first letter of each line in order on the center blanks.

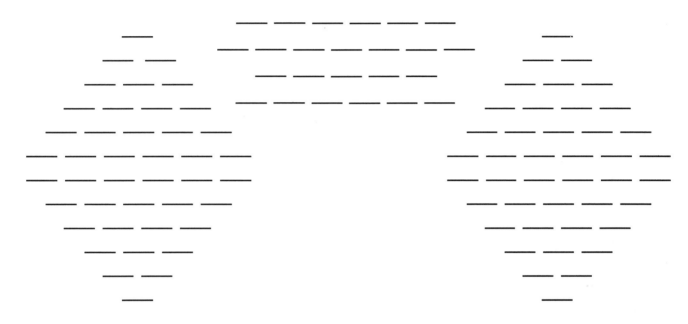

Left

1. 4th letter of the alphabet
2. abbreviation for Oklahoma
3. taxi
4. a piece of work someone must do
5. to command
6. a place of safety
7. to feel a light itch
8. to lift or raise, especially by using a rope
9. a long, serious poem that tells a story about a hero
10. used to row a boat
11. abbreviation for *doctor*
12. 4th vowel of the alphabet

Right

1. 18th letter of the alphabet
2. after all
3. fried or scrambled
4. to strongly encourage to do something
5. to burn with hot liquid
6. rarely
7. a feeling of resentment
8. to avoid being caught
9. homophone for *I'll*
10. homophone for *sow*
11. To take what has been given is to rec __ __ ve.
12. 12th letter of the alphabet

Name _____

ar sound

Music to Our Ears

March 3 is National Anthem Day. On this day in 1931, the United States Senate and President Herbert Hoover signed the bill that made "The Star-Spangled Banner" our national anthem.

Banner has the *ər* sound. This sound can have many different spellings. Write words with this sound using the letter groups listed and the clues. Each letter group will be used only once.

or	bu	yo	su	te	la	tu	de
ad	ir	at	ul	ve	al	rt	te
pe	en	ar	ca	rn	bu	en	ac
er	ra	po	fr	ca			

1. to give up ☐ __ **r r** __ __ **d** __ ☐

2. correct __ __ **c u** __ __ __ __

3. thief __ __ **r g** __ __ **r**

4. a device that can solve math problems ☐☐ **l c** __ __ **a t** __ __

5. a heavy load __ __ __ **r d** ☐ __

6. very well liked __ __ **p u l** __ __ __

7. soft food made from fermented milk ☐☐ **g u** __ __ __

8. a break ☐ __ **a c** ☐ __ **r e**

9. first one then the other __ __ __ **t e** __ ☐ **a** __ __ __

10. one who has lost hope __ __ **s** __ __ __ **r** __ ☐ **e**

11. a cave ☐ __ __ __ __ **r n**

12. commanding officer of a navy __ __ __ **m** ☐ __ **a l**

To find out who wrote the words to our national anthem, unscramble the boxed letters. Hint: One letter is not boxed.

__ __ __ __ __ __ __   __ __ __ __ **K** __ __

Name _____

A Great Group of Girls

Juliette Low founded the Girl Scout movement in America on March 12, 1912. It is the world's largest voluntary organization for girls and women. Girl Scout Week, held the week that includes March 12, honors the first Girl Scout troop meeting.

In the United States, the Girl Scout Promise includes service in three areas. To determine these three areas, read each clue and write the answer in the puzzle. Then, write the outside letter of each word in numerical order on the blanks.

1. ___ ___ ___   2. ___ ___ ___ ___ ___ ___   3. ___ ___ ___ ___ ___ ___ ___

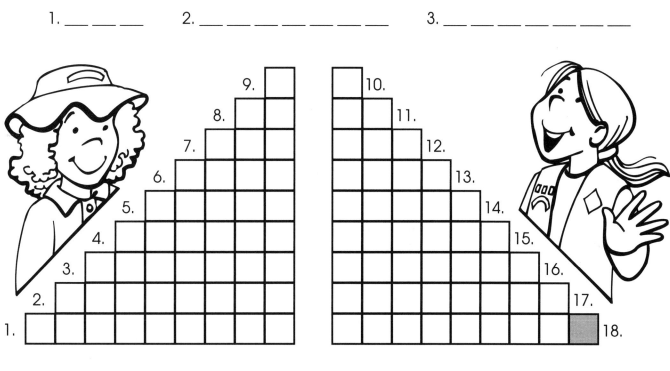

1. confused talk that does not mean anything
2. something that prevents one from moving forward
3. to lose hope
4. cold and damp
5. place where there is water in an otherwise dry area
6. a single person or group
7. to pinch, squeeze, or bite
8. abbreviation for Tennessee

9. 18th letter of the alphabet
10. 25th letter of the alphabet
11. contraction for *I am*
12. homophone for *tee*
13. to shock in a deep way
14. a long, wide, thick board
15. a two-piece bathing suit
16. line in the distance where sky meets sea or land
17. heavy snowstorm with strong winds
18. to hold back; to keep under control

Albert Einstein's Birthday

Name _____

Great with Numbers

Albert Einstein was born on March 14, 1879. He was one of the greatest scientists of all time. He is best known for his theory of relativity, which he developed through deep philosophical thought and complex mathematical reasoning.

Complete the puzzle with words containing one of these number prefixes: *uni*—one, *bi*—two, *tri*—three, *mono*—one.

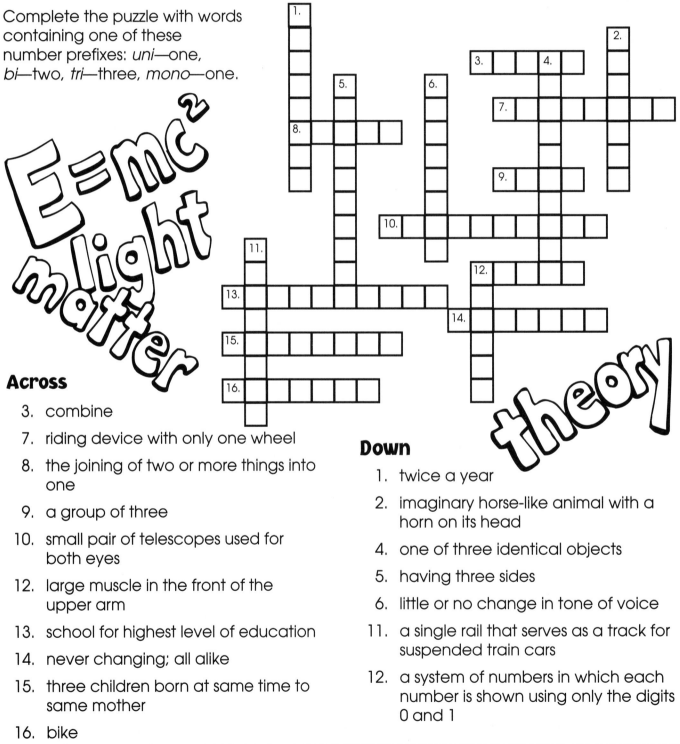

Across

3. combine
7. riding device with only one wheel
8. the joining of two or more things into one
9. a group of three
10. small pair of telescopes used for both eyes
12. large muscle in the front of the upper arm
13. school for highest level of education
14. never changing; all alike
15. three children born at same time to same mother
16. bike

Down

1. twice a year
2. imaginary horse-like animal with a horn on its head
4. one of three identical objects
5. having three sides
6. little or no change in tone of voice
11. a single rail that serves as a track for suspended train cars
12. a system of numbers in which each number is shown using only the digits 0 and 1

frequently misspelled words

U.S. Military Academy Founded

Name ____

Be Careful, Colonel!

The U.S. Military Academy at West Point, New Jersey, is the oldest military college in the world. It was founded on March 16, 1802.

A *colonel* is a military officer. A *kernel* is a grain or seed. These two words sound the same but are spelled differently. Words like this are often misspelled, as are words with silent letters, such as *taupe*. Write a word in the boxes for each clue. Be careful! Some words are tricky. To help you, the letters spelling the name of the man who invented X-rays have been provided. His birthday is March 27, 1845.

1. one after eleventh
2. 5-cent coin
3. person who serves in the army
4. super; fantastic
5. chief law officer of a county
6. fenced-in place for horses
7. to make someone feel uncomfortable
8. to give advice; suggest
9. from another country
10. muscle used to taste
11. something that occurs
12. an after-dinner treat
13. a noncommissioned officer in the armed forces
14. odd or eccentric
15. a slipper made of soft leather and without a heel

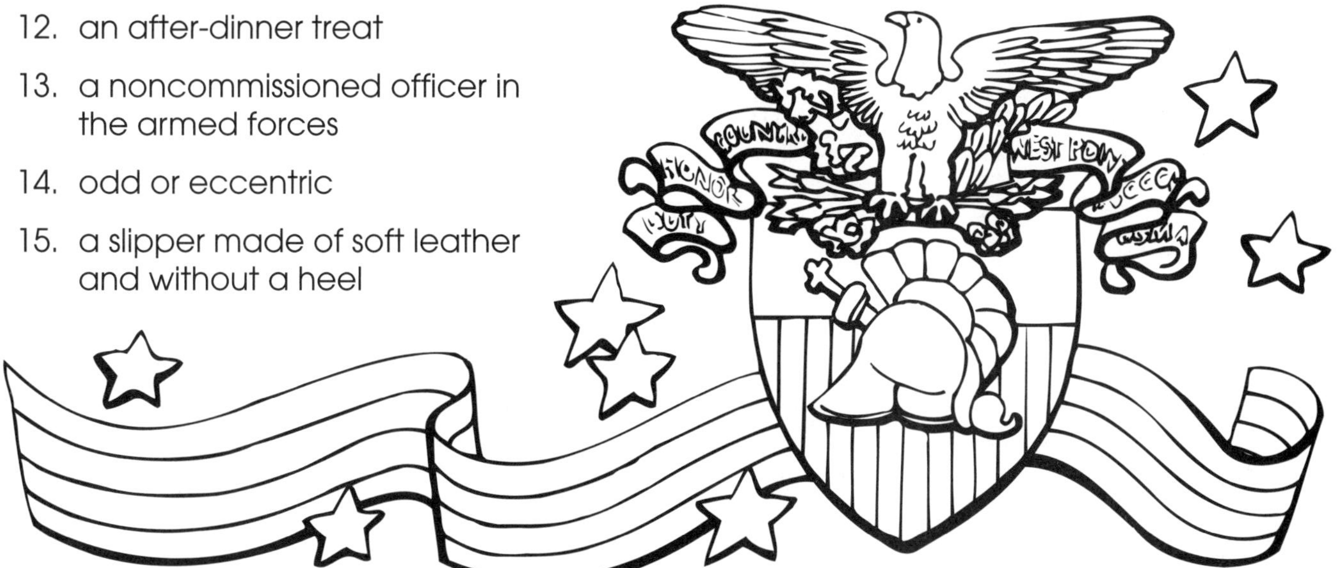

Name _____

Eat Smart

March is National Nutrition Month. It emphasizes the importance of good nutrition.

All of the words listed can be categorized according to the food groups in the food pyramid. One group has been left out. To learn about the missing group, write each word under the correct category and cross it off. Then, write the remaining words in order on the lines.

_____ _____ , _____ , and _____ _____ .

Use	turkey	crackers	fats	kiwi
broccoli	pumpernickel	Swiss cheese	nectarines	cottage cheese
rye	strawberries	oils	wheat	salmon
cheese	sweets	onion	squash	milk
pecans	tuna	chicken	spaghetti	yogurt
apples	cabbage	banana	carrots	sparingly

Vegetables	Meat, Fish, Nuts	Fruit	Breads, Rice, Pasta	Dairy

Let There Be Peace!

The Peace Corps was created by the U.S. government to help people in developing countries improve their living conditions. It was established in March 1961. Two of the three goals of this organization are to help the poor obtain everyday needs and to increase understanding between people of other countries and Americans. To determine the third goal, complete each analogy. Then, use the number code to fill in the boxes.

```
|   |   |   |   |   |   |   |   |   |   |   |   |   |   |   |   |   |   |   |
  1   2     3   4   5   6   7   8   9    10  11  12  13  14    15  16  17  18  19
```

1. Atlantic Ocean is to Puerto Rico as Pacific Ocean is to __ __ __ __ .
            5 17

2. Rocky Mountains is to United States as Andes Mountains is to

   __ __ __ __ __ __ __ .
   17 4   9   1   17

3. Sudan is to the Red Sea as Italy is to the __ __ __ __ __ __ __ __ __ __ __ __ Sea.
            6 9 14   8 19 4 12 17 16 17

4. Tokyo is to Japan as Geneva is to __ __ __ __ __ __ __ __ __ .
            10 1 16 4 13 17 14

5. Zaire is to Africa as Spain is to __ __ __ __ __ __ .
            9 12 2 15 19

6. Acapulco, Mexico, is to Pacific as Miami, Florida, is to __ __ __ __ __ __ __ .
            17 1 13 17 8 18

7. Canada is to provinces as Australia is to __ __ __ __ __ __ .
            8 17 1 19

8. United States is to English as Latin America is to __ __ __ __ __ __ __ .
            15 17

9. Poland is to Eastern Europe as Belgium is to __ __ __ __ __ __ __ __ __ __ __ __ .
            10   19 4   9   7 3 16

10. Nepal is to Mount Everest as Alaska is to __ __ __ __ __ __ __ __ __ __ __ .
             6 11 8 6   13 19

11. Texas is to Mexico as Minnesota is to __ __ __ __ __ __ .
             18 17 17 14 17

12. Tennessee is to United States as Queensland is to __ __ __ __ __ __ __ __ .
             17   1 4 17 13 17

National
Women's
History
Month

Name _____

Wonderful Women

March is a time to honor the many contributions and achievements women have made to society. It is National Women's History Month. During this month, women like Harriet Tubman, who led more than 300 slaves to freedom via the Underground Railroad, and Eleanor Roosevelt, who wrote a daily newspaper column when she was First Lady, are recognized.

Contributions contains the ü sound. Read each phonetic spelling with the ü sound. Then, circle the word for each phonetic spelling in the puzzle. The words appear horizontally, vertically, and diagonally.

'sü-və-ˌnir	'dü-pli-kət	'grüp	'yün-yən	i-'lü-mə-nət	'yüth
im-'prüv	'nü-sᵉn(t)s	ˌən-'rü-lē	ba-'bün	kən-'süm	'sü-tə-bəl
rü-'tēn	'shrüd	'sä-lə-ˌtüd	krü-'sād-ər	kə-'kün	kə-'büs
'nüm-rəs	'nüz-ˌstand	'kar-ə-ˌbü	här-'pün	'jü-əl-rē	lə-'gün
'lüs	'thrü	'smüth	kär-'tün	'büst	'nü-trəl

```
c n r a n u m e r o u s s c c h
a e e l c a m u y r s o m n r t
b i s w k u n o o u n i o n u h
o b o o s t o b u w l m o u s r
o n a n s s r i t h a p t i a o
s e o m g o t r h t g r h s d u
e c e h e r h a r p o o n a e g
l c r t o b o c n f o v t n r h
y o h c a e e u n d n e v c i e
r c n b r n o n p m e n t e a l
l o o l y r i n e v u o s l s b
e o o o l m o m b a b o o n h a
w n t o u p e d u t i l o s r t
e s r s r t d u p l i c a t e i
j c a e n e u t r a l i d e w u
s b c o u x t r o u t i n e d s
```

Name _____

1-2-3, Jump!

Albert Berry from Missouri made the first parachute jump out of an airplane in March of 1912. What an accomplishment!

Use the clues and the letters in *parachute* and *accomplishment* to write words in each puzzle.

parachute

1. a hollow muscle that pumps blood
2. a box made of wooden slats
3. a khaki, brownish color
4. to act dishonestly
5. a map used for guiding an aircraft
6. a piece of cloth used to mend a hole
7. a round, orange-yellow fuzzy fruit
8. inexpensive
9. to get to
10. a section in a book

accomplishment

1. to put in charge or trust; entrust
2. having to do with the mind
3. ill will
4. the structure surrounding a fireplace
5. an observation or remark
6. to gather or collect
7. weather conditions of a place
8. small car
9. really funny
10. garments
11. to begin

Unscramble the letters in the shaded boxes to discover the famous Italian artist who was born on March 6, 1475.

___ ___ ___ ___ ___ ___ ___ g ___ ___ ___

Name _____

Money Matters

The first federal U.S. mint was established in Philadelphia on April 2, 1792. This was almost 20 years after Congress first printed paper money.

To learn more about the history of currency in our country, write a word on the blanks for each clue. Then, use the number code to write words in the boxes relating to U.S. currency.

| 1 | 2 | 3 | 4 | 5 | 6 | 7 | 8 | 9 | 10 | 11 | 12 |

were paper money issued by Congress to help finance the Revolutionary War, which began April 19, 1775 and ended April 15, 1783.

a customer ___ ___ ___ ___ ___ ___
1 11 5   7   8   4

not changing ___ ___ ___ ___ ___ ___ ___ ___
1   2   3   12   9   10   6   4

a thin, flat piece cut from something ___ ___ ___ ___ ___
12 11   5   1   7

not fresh ___ ___ ___ ___ ___
12   9 10 11   7

| 1 | 2 | 3 | 4 | 5 | 6 | 7 | 8 | 9 | 10 |

were paper money issued during the Civil War. They were printed in green. The Civil War began April 12, 1861.

a surface on a TV used to show pictures ___ ___ ___ ___ ___ ___
10   8   2   4   3   5

a short prayer giving thanks for a meal ___ ___ ___ ___ ___
1   2   7   8   4

melted fat ___ ___ ___ ___ ___ ___
1   2   4   7   10   3

to fracture ___ ___ ___ ___ ___
6   2   3   7   9

| 1 | 2 | 3 | 4 | 5 | | 6 | 7 | 8 | 9 | 10 | 11 |

is what the U.S. government declared greenbacks to be. This is money people must accept in payment of debts.

risk; harm ___ ___ ___ ___ ___ ___
9   4   8   3   2   11

where flowers grow ___ ___ ___ ___ ___ ___
3   4   11   9 10   8

royal ___ ___ ___ ___ ___
11   7   3   4   1

to become knotted or mixed up ___ ___ ___ ___ ___ ___ ___
6   4   8   3   5   2   9

National Sports Safety Month

Name _____

Safety First

Sports are great for kids of all ages. However, it is important to take each sport seriously and to follow all of the safety rules involved when participating. This is why April is National Sports Safety Month.

It is important that all athletes wear protective equipment to help prevent injuries. Complete each word below with the correct letter. Be careful! More than one letter can complete some words. Then, write the letters on the blanks using the number code to see some important protective equipment that makes sports activities safer.

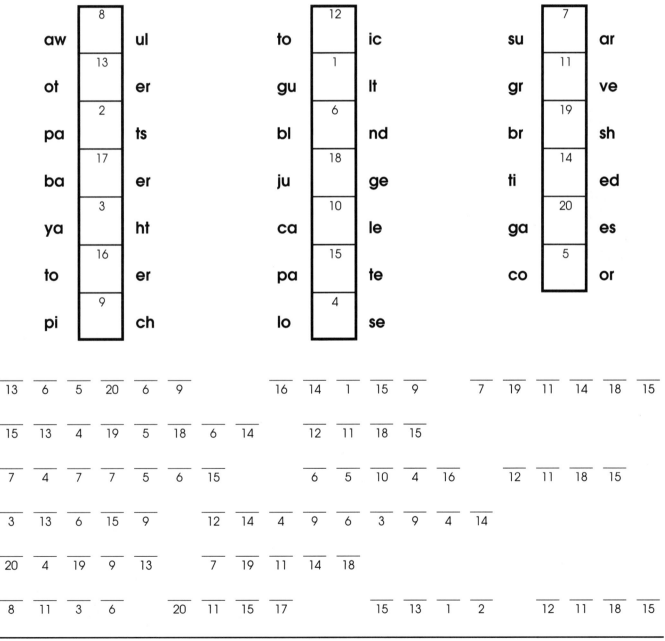

aw	8	ul
ot	13	er
pa	2	ts
ba	17	er
ya	3	ht
to	16	er
pi	9	ch

to	12	ic
gu	1	lt
bl	6	nd
ju	18	ge
ca	10	le
pa	15	te
lo	4	se

su	7	ar
gr	11	ve
br	19	sh
ti	14	ed
ga	20	es
co	5	or

___ ___ ___ ___ ___ ___
13 6   5   20 6   9

___ ___ ___ ___ ___
16 14 1   15 9

___ ___ ___ ___ ___ ___ ___
7   19 11 14 18 15

___ ___ ___ ___ ___ ___ ___ ___
15 13 4   19 5   18 6   14

___ ___ ___ ___
12 11 18 15

___ ___ ___ ___ ___ ___ ___
7   4   7   7   5   6   15

___ ___ ___ ___ ___
6   5   10 4   16

___ ___ ___ ___
12 11 18 15

___ ___ ___ ___ ___
3   13 6   15 9

___ ___ ___ ___ ___ ___ ___ ___ ___
12 14 4   9   6   3   9   4   14

___ ___ ___ ___ ___
20 4   19 9   13

___ ___ ___ ___ ___
7   19 11 14 18

___ ___ ___ ___
8   11 3   6

___ ___ ___ ___
20 11 15 17

___ ___ ___ ___
15 13 1   2

___ ___ ___ ___
12 11 18 15

73

Word Games: Grades 5–6

Name _____

Help Others

National Volunteer Week is held the third full week in April. It promotes the value of volunteering in communities around the country. There are many ways volunteers can help others. Community volunteering is a rewarding experience.

Experience ends in *-ence*, meaning *act, condition,* or *quality.* Use each clue to write a word ending in *-ence* or *-ance* in the boxes. Then, use the number code to complete the puzzle to learn about one man's contributions to society.

1. ability to hold up under hardship, strain, or pain

   ☐☐☐☐☐☐☐☐☐☐
   ͏͏15͏͏͏͏͏͏͏͏32͏͏13

2. act of opposing a powerful person

   ☐☐☐☐☐☐☐☐
   ͏͏16͏͏͏͏10

3. the way a person looks

   ☐☐☐☐☐☐☐☐☐☐
   ͏͏27͏͏35͏͏͏͏28

4. the power to withstand

   ☐☐☐☐☐☐☐☐
   ͏͏36͏͏31͏͏19͏͏23

5. ability to learn and understand

   ☐☐☐☐☐☐☐☐☐☐☐☐
   ͏͏9͏͏29͏͏2͏͏3͏͏1

6. someone you know but not very well

   ☐☐☐☐☐☐☐☐☐☐☐☐
   ͏͏20͏͏͏͏12͏͏34͏͏4͏͏͏͏17

7. lack of knowledge or education

   ☐☐☐☐☐☐☐☐☐
   ͏͏26͏͏11

8. something that saves time and work

   ☐☐☐☐☐☐☐☐☐☐☐
   ͏͏25͏͏͏͏24

9. leadership

   ☐☐☐☐☐☐☐☐
   ͏͏37͏͏14

10. a great supply

    ☐☐☐☐☐☐☐☐☐
    ͏͏22͏͏6͏͏33͏͏5

11. the act of staying away from

    ☐☐☐☐☐☐☐☐☐
    ͏͏30͏͏21͏͏8

12. conformity in fulfilling a requirement

    ☐☐☐☐☐☐☐☐☐☐
    ͏͏7͏͏͏͏18

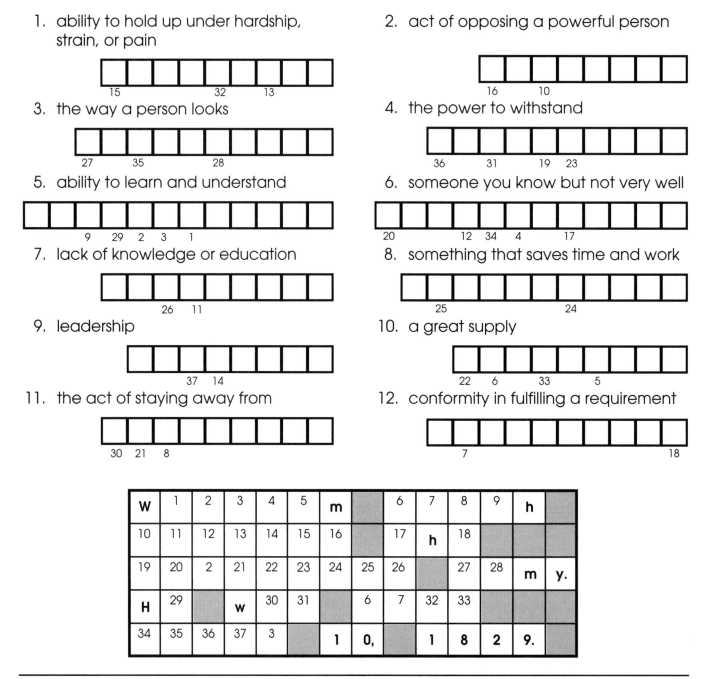

w	1	2	3	4	5	m		6	7	8	9	h	
10	11	12	13	14	15	16		17	h	18			
19	20	2	21	22	23	24	25	26		27	28	m	y.
H	29		w	30	31		6	7	32	33			
34	35	36	37	3		1	0,		1	8	2	9.	

Name ____

A Tragedy

April 14, 1865 was a sad day in our nation's history. On this day, President Abraham Lincoln was shot in Ford's Theater.

Using the letters in the name of Lincoln's assassin, complete each word by choosing two two-letter pairs. Each pair can be used only once.

nd	ig	ou	ty	lt	of
er	dy	gh	en	je	om
el	ld	ct	es	te	le
it	sh	ht	et	ck	na
se	rs	ce	aw	ub	ow

1.	o	b		**J**			
2.	p	r		**o**			
3.	d	i		**h**			
4.	d	o		**n**			
5.	d	r		**W**			
6.	w	e		**i**			
7.	s	e		**l**			
8.	j	a		**k**			
9.	a	s		**e**			
10.	m	o		**s**			
11.	d	o		**B**			
12.	b	r		**o**			
13.	c	l		**o**			
14.	m	o		**t**			
15.	e	i		**h**			

Name _____

An Unforgettable Day

An unforgettable historical April event has fascinated America and much of the world for years. Books and movies have been created to help people learn about this tragedy. This event occurred on April 15, 1912.

To find out what occurred, read each clue and write the answer on the blanks. Then, write the first letter of each line in order on the blanks below.

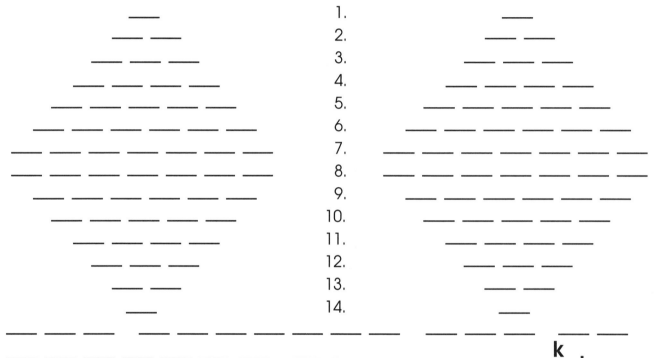

Left

1. first letter for a brewed drink served with ice and lemon
2. hello
3. Environmental Protection Agency
4. homophone for *tail*
5. opposite of *outer*
6. game played with rackets
7. to desert
8. antonym for *nice*
9. piece of land surrounded by water
10. antonym for *kind*
11. homophone for *whole*
12. frozen water
13. seventh note on a musical scale
14. first vowel in the alphabet

Right

1. 14th letter of the alphabet
2. antonym for *out*
3. hat
4. homophone for *urn*
5. antonym for *destroy*
6. antonym for *import*
7. a regular way of doing something
8. faint, unsteady light
9. antonym for *lazy*
10. antonym for *quiet*
11. the bird of peace
12. homophone for *sun*
13. abbreviation for Alaska
14. 14th letter of the alphabet

Name _____

Be Kind to Our Earth!

Earth Day is held on April 22 to encourage people to protect the environment. It was first observed in 1970. To learn three different ways to help the environment, write a word in the boxes for each clue. The shaded letters will spell the answers.

1. gases sprayed under pressure to create a fine mist or spray

2. used gas released from a car

3. a pollution that includes loud music and jet airplanes (2 words)

4. reduce this by taking shorter showers (2 words)

5. conserve this by turning off lights and fans

6. conserve this by walking somewhere

7. a greasy liquid that is put in a car (2 words)

8. full of information— published daily

9. containers that milk comes in

10. metal containers of soda, root beer, and other carbonated beverages (2 words)

11. a very thin sheet of metal (2 words)

12. a group of sheets of paper, bound on one side, that contains a huge list of people's names, addresses, and phone numbers (2 words)

13. device used to renew a cell phone's battery

14. disposable paper drinking containers (2 words)

15. another word for *car*

16. grocery bags not made of paper

17. plastic containers of water (2 words)

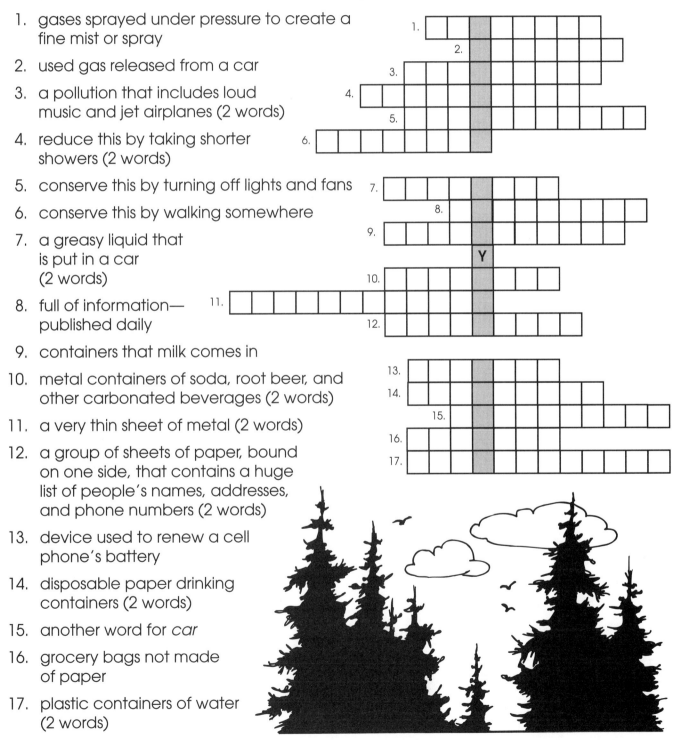

Sky Awareness Week

Name _____

Check Out the Sky!

Sky Awareness Week is held the last full week in April. It was created to encourage people to learn to "read" the sky: its natural beauty, its protection, the weather, and sun safety.

Complete the puzzle with words that pertain to the sky.

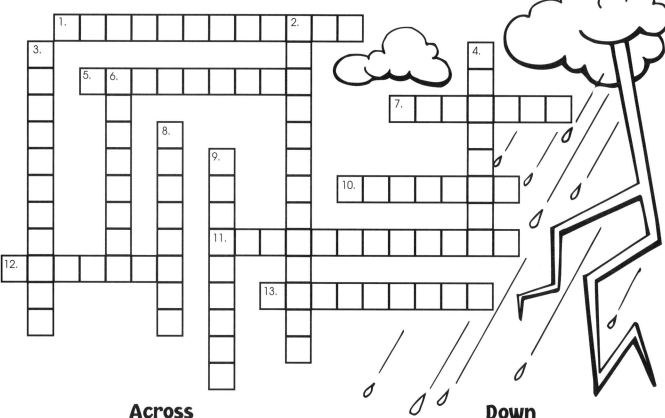

Across

1. when Earth passes between the sun and the moon (2 words)

5. a very strong windstorm in which wind blows at 74 mph or more

7. the rising of the sun each day

10. formed when white light from the sun passes through raindrops

11. when the moon passes between the sun and Earth (2 words)

12. a destructive, funnel-shaped cloud

13. electricity from cloud to cloud or cloud to ground

Down

2. rain, snow, or other moisture that falls from the sky

3. flash of lightning and the thunder that follows

4. gases, sprayed under pressure to create a fine spray, that damage the ozone layer

6. used for protection against precipitation

8. a lotion that helps prevent sunburn

9. an illness caused by being out in the sun too long

Name _____

Marvelous Math

"If you can do math, you can do anything!" That statement is the focus of Mathematics Education Month, which is celebrated in April.

Circle each mathematical word from the Word Bank in the puzzle. Words appear horizontally, vertically, and diagonally.

Word Bank

quotient	addition	dividend	trapezoid	area
radius	remainder	calculate	sum	difference
geometry	fraction	perimeter	algebra	multiplication
numerator	reduce	circumference	product	

```
d  r  c  i  t  n  o  i  t  c  a  r  f  o  s  t
l  n  d  i  f  f  e  r  e  n  c  e  q  g  g  h
e  o  r  t  r  a  p  e  z  o  i  d  u  e  r  m
x  i  s  e  p  c  u  p  l  s  l  b  o  o  d  d
r  t  a  m  c  t  u  p  u  f  o  d  t  m  i  a
m  a  o  r  r  i  m  l  t  m  a  i  e  v  r
t  c  n  e  e  m  r  t  f  i  r  a  e  t  i  b
s  i  o  p  d  a  u  e  m  e  d  s  n  r  d  e
l  l  i  g  u  k  a  b  m  r  r  y  t  y  e  g
g  p  t  c  c  r  f  u  o  a  f  e  z  l  n  l
c  i  i  l  e  g  n  x  l  d  i  t  n  m  d  a
p  t  d  g  a  e  n  r  o  i  b  n  s  c  a  w
a  l  d  c  i  p  r  o  d  u  c  t  d  e  e  r
g  u  a  n  a  n  i  f  n  s  a  c  i  e  r  e
n  m  a  n  e  t  a  l  u  c  l  a  c  a  r  m
a  g  p  e  r  i  m  e  t  e  r  r  o  m  p  j
```

Name _____

First Book of Stamps Issued

The Mail Will Make It

The U.S. Postal Service issued its first book of stamps in April 1900. Each stamp cost 2¢. Forty years earlier, another big April event occurred in the postal industry. To find out what this event was, write an answer in the boxes for each clue. Each answer will go one letter past the next number. This is because each new word begins with the last two letters of the word before it. The first one has been done for you. Then, write the circled letters in order on the blanks. Determine and write the missing letters in the boxes.

The ___ ___ ___ ☐ ___☐☐___☐___ ___ ___ ___☐___☐☐ began.

1. to fasten together
2. great beauty or magnificence
3. to create; to begin
4. surface features of an area of land
5. to demand strongly
6. a bad smell; rhymes with *wrench*
7. a hard task
8. authentic, real
9. to arrange by talking about
10. stretched the tightest
11. firm or fixed; loyal
12. to make more active
13. short and to the point; rhymes with *verse*
14. stimulation of a sense organ

Crossword grid:
1. c l a s p 2.s 3. 4. 5. 6. 7. 8. 9. 10. 11. 12. 13. 14.

Name _____

How Does Your Garden Grow?

National Garden Week is in April. What a perfect time to get out and plant!

Use the garden full of letters to help determine the plant-related words below. Go across, then down.

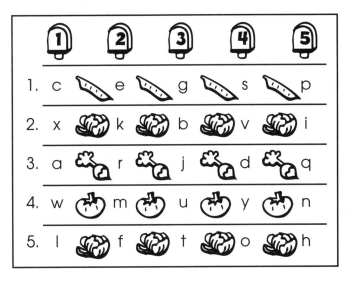

1. a tough, nonliving material that acts like an outside skeleton for each plant cell

   ___ ___ ___ ___   ___ ___ ___ ___
   1-1 2-1 1-5 1-5   1-4 1-3 1-5 1-5

2. an organelle that makes sugars using carbon dioxide, water, and the energy from sunlight ___ ___ ___ ___ ___ ___ ___ ___ ___ ___ ___
                      1-1 5-5 1-5 4-5 2-3 4-5 5-1 1-5 1-3 4-1 3-5

3. a green substance in the chloroplasts that traps energy from sunlight

   ___ ___ ___ ___ ___ ___ ___ ___ ___ ___ ___
   1-1 5-5 1-5 4-5 2-3 4-5 5-1 5-5 4-4 1-5 1-5

4. a plant with long tubes inside that carry food and water to all parts of the plant

   ___ ___ ___ ___ ___ ___ ___ ___   ___ ___ ___ ___ ___
   4-2 1-3 4-1 1-1 3-4 1-5 1-3 2-3   5-1 1-5 1-3 5-4 3-5

5. an evergreen plant ___ ___ ___ ___ ___ ___ ___
                      1-1 4-5 5-4 5-2 2-5 2-1 2-3

6. flowerless, seedless plants that are vascular plants ___ ___ ___ ___ ___
                                                        2-5 2-1 2-3 5-4 4-1

7. nonvascular plants with no roots or leaves ___ ___ ___ ___ ___ ___
                                              2-4 4-5 4-1 4-1 2-1 4-1

8. vascular plants with flowers from which fruits and seeds develop

   ___ ___ ___ ___ ___ ___ ___ ___ ___   ___ ___ ___ ___ ___ ___
   2-5 1-5 4-5 1-4 2-1 2-3 5-2 5-4 3-1   5-1 1-5 1-3 5-4 3-5 4-1

9. the two main groups of flowering plants ___ ___ ___ ___ ___ ___ ___ ___
                                           2-4 4-5 5-4 4-5 1-1 4-5 3-5 4-1

   (one seed leaf) and ___ ___ ___ ___ ___ ___ (two seed leaves)
                       4-3 5-2 1-1 4-5 3-5 4-1

vocabulary

First
American
Medical
School
Opens

Name _____

Opportunities for All

On May 5, 1765, the first American medical school opened. On May 19, 1795, an American philanthropist was born. This generous man left $7 million to establish a now well-known university and hospital.

To find out his name, write a word in the boxes for each clue. Each answer will go one letter past the next number. This is because each new word begins with the last two letters of the word before it. When the puzzle is complete, write the shaded letters in order.

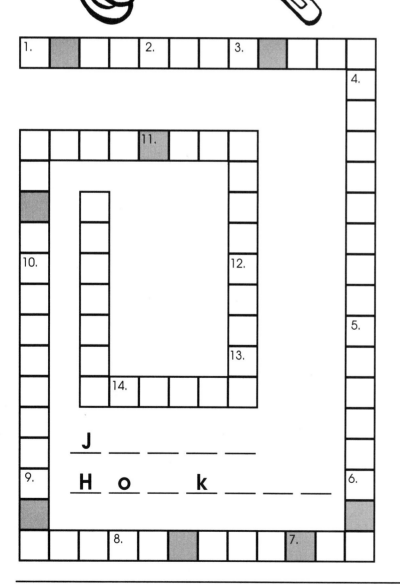

1. round, red fruit eaten as a vegetable

2. a white bony object that grows from your jaw

3. a small, metal or plastic cap used in sewing

4. lawful

5. ground or land

6. to swarm in or over in a way that harms or bothers

7. a sudden rush of people or animals in one direction

8. to fool or trick

9. able to do a number of things well

10. in the direction of the length

11. a feeling of great excitement

12. start

13. lasting forever

14. in spite of the fact that

Name _____

Teachers Are Terrific!

National Teacher Day is observed on the Tuesday during Teacher Appreciation Week. This week takes place the first full week in May. Remember to do something nice for all the dedicated teachers who devote their lives to helping you learn!

Complete the puzzle using words that relate to teachers and school.

Across

3. to refuse to give up despite difficulties
6. to gather all of one's thoughts or efforts
8. good chance
9. to keep in mind; to remember
10. providing information; instructive
11. to call for skill, effort, or imagination
12. good opinion; high regard of self

Down

1. the act of promoting and motivating
2. to be better or greater than others
4. remarkable; not ordinary
5. to take part in a contest
7. having imagination and ability

Name _____

Marvelous Moms

Mother's Day is held the second Sunday in May to honor mothers. It became a public holiday on May 9, 1914.

Write a word for each clue in the boxes. Each word uses letters from the word *compassionate*. Then, read the message in the shaded boxes.

1. condition of suddenly forgetting some or all of the past

2. rock

3. strength to carry on or last

4. sea

5. to be made up of

6. a substance used in puddings; contains starch from a tropical plant

7. the backbone

8. a dirty or colored spot

9. to give approval

10. to create or write

11. a spoon used to stir tea or coffee

12. a valuable thing to have

Name _____

Many Good Deeds

Clara Barton was an American nurse who devoted her life to the good of humanity. She founded the American Red Cross on May 21, 1881. Barton earned an interesting nickname while working with wounded men during the Civil War. To find out this nickname, write the answer to each clue. All answers end in *-ity,* as in *humanity,* or *-y.* The shaded boxes will spell her nickname.

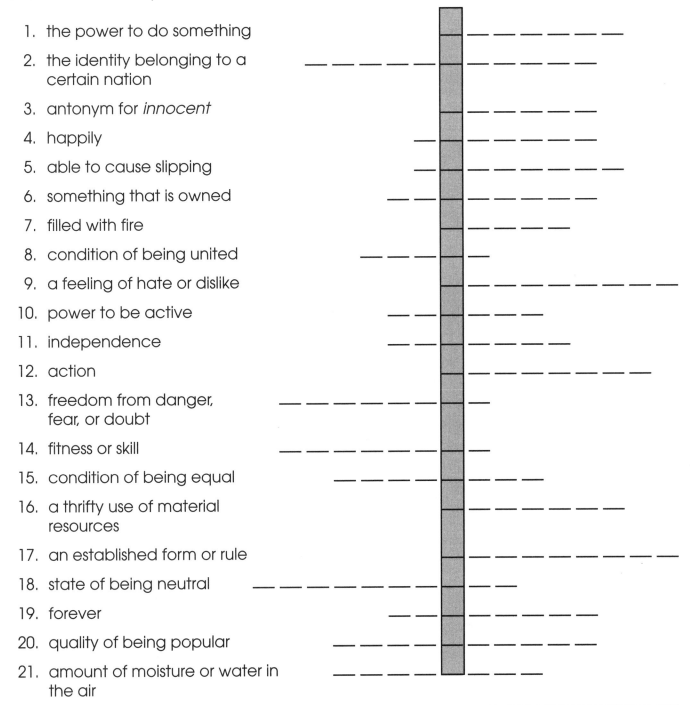

1. the power to do something
2. the identity belonging to a certain nation
3. antonym for *innocent*
4. happily
5. able to cause slipping
6. something that is owned
7. filled with fire
8. condition of being united
9. a feeling of hate or dislike
10. power to be active
11. independence
12. action
13. freedom from danger, fear, or doubt
14. fitness or skill
15. condition of being equal
16. a thrifty use of material resources
17. an established form or rule
18. state of being neutral
19. forever
20. quality of being popular
21. amount of moisture or water in the air

Golden Gate Bridge Opens

Name _____

A Great Big Bridge

On May 27, 1937, the spectacular Golden Gate Bridge in San Francisco opened.

To find out another famous landmark that opened on May 1, 1931, write an antonym for each word in the boxes. Then, use the number code to fill in the blanks.

___ ___ ___   ___ ___ ___ ___ ___ ___
1   2   3   4   5   6   7   8   9

___ ___ ___ ___ ___   ___ ___ ___ ___ ___ ___ ___ ___
10   11   12   13   14   15   16   17   18   19   20   21   22

inhale   ☐☐☐☐☐☐
   3   2   12   18   9

rigid   ☐☐☐☐☐☐☐☐
   18   4   7   15   18   4

after   ☐☐☐☐☐☐
  15   3   8   3

neat   ☐☐☐☐
  5   14   10   10

lowered   ☐☐☐☐☐☐
  18   17   13   3   19

deep   ☐☐☐☐☐
  10   2   12   18   18

deflate   ☐☐☐☐☐☐☐
  17   21   18   12   13   9

loss   ☐☐☐☐
   7   11   8

incorrect   ☐☐☐☐☐☐☐
  12   16   8   12   1   4

clean   ☐☐☐☐☐
  19   20   8   11

full   ☐☐☐☐
  3   5   6   13

noisy   ☐☐☐☐
  16   7   9   1

sickly   ☐☐☐☐☐☐
  2   14   12   18   13   2

break   ☐☐☐☐☐☐
  8   4   6   12   17   8

vertical   ☐☐☐☐☐☐☐☐☐☐
  2   8   20   21   13   12   18

mobile   ☐☐☐☐☐☐☐☐
  10   11   12   13   17   21   12   8

pessimistic   ☐☐☐☐☐☐☐☐☐
   6   11   7   5   20   10   13   17

energetic   ☐☐☐☐☐☐☐
   12   1   7   22   16   4   19

cry   ☐☐☐☐☐
  18   12   16   22   2

same   ☐☐☐☐☐☐☐☐☐
  19   20   14   8   9   21   11

Name _____

A Famous President

A well-loved and well-remembered president was born in May. Write an answer in the puzzle for each clue. Then, write the outside letters in numerical order on the blanks to learn who this president is.

__ • __ • __ __ __ __ __ __ __   __ __ __ __ __ __ __
 1   2   3   4   5   6   7   8   9   10 11 12 13 14 15 16

on May 29, 1917.

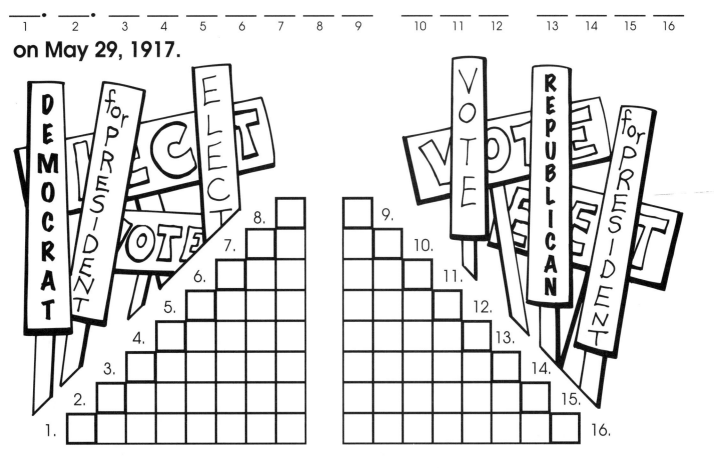

1. a great danger or risk; a TV show
2. to complete an obligation
3. a metal container for boiling or cooking
4. to do well; to be better than others
5. a person, place, or thing
6. homophone for *knew*
7. two letters used to form the past tense of many verbs
8. fourth letter of the alphabet

9. 25th letter of the alphabet
10. abbreviation for *Volkswagen*
11. homophone for *see*
12. antonym for *fail*
13. a short finger; the two you have are opposable
14. cape; sleeveless coat
15. a knitted pullover worn in the winter
16. to serve a purpose

prefixes pro-, pre-, and post-

Memorial
Day

Memorial Day

The last Monday in May, Memorial Day, is set aside to honor Americans who have given their lives for our country. These brave men and women died to protect our freedom.

Protect contains the prefix *pro-*, meaning *for* or *in favor of*. Two other prefixes are *pre-*, meaning *before*, and *post-*, meaning *after*. Write a word beginning with one of these prefixes in the boxes for each definition. Then, use the number code to finish the sentences.

1. to say or speak correctly

   40 14 23 33 34 1 15 44 39

2. happening before the usual or proper time

   40 7 37 32 28 29 41 38 20

3. to make or get ready

   40 22 27 40 4 7 25

4. an advance showing or viewing

   40 38 10 3 31 5

5. a note added to a completed letter

   40 13 12 30 19 44 7 43 40 24

6. a plan of procedure

   40 22 9 22 28 16

7. to arrange beforehand

   40 22 39 6 7 14 6 33 37

8. a particular way of doing something

   40 14 23 44 31 8 41 38 27

9. the introductory remarks of a writer

   40 7 25 35 6 44 20

10. the descendants from one generation

    40 13 12 36 10 14 3 26 18

11. an official public announcement

    40 38 9 44 2 17 16 11 24 43 23 15

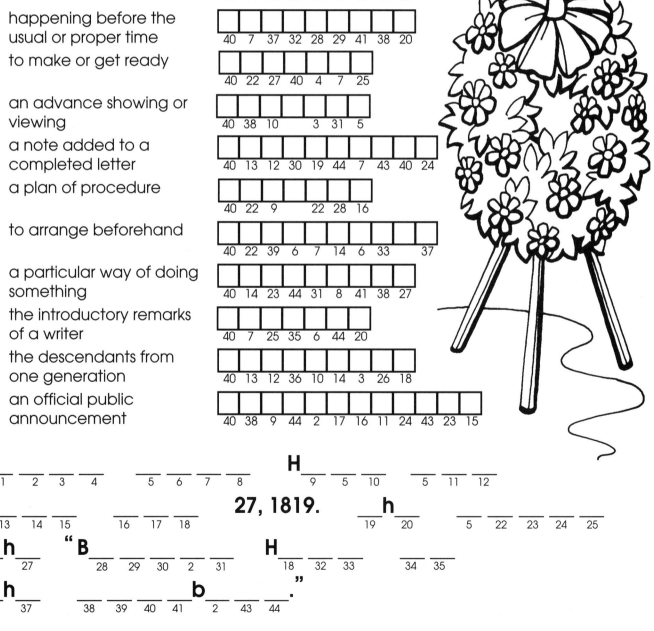

J _ _ _ _   _ _ _ _   H _ _ _   _ _ _
  1 2 3 4   5 6 7 8   9 5 10   5 11 12

b _ _ _   _ _ _   27, 1819.   _ h _   _ _ _ _ _ _ _
  13 14 15 16 17 18   19 20   5 22 23 24 25

_ h _   " B _ _ _ _ _   H _ _ _   _ _ _
26 27   28 29 30 2 31   18 32 33   34 35

_ h _   _ _ _ _ _ b _ _ _ ."
36 37   38 39 40 41 2 43 44

National Physical Fitness and Sports Month

analogies

Name _____

Get Moving!

Get out there and exercise! May is the perfect month to get involved in some kind of physical activity or sport because it is National Physical Fitness and Sports Month.

Complete each analogy with the scrambled word. Then, use the number code to finish the message about another special May event.

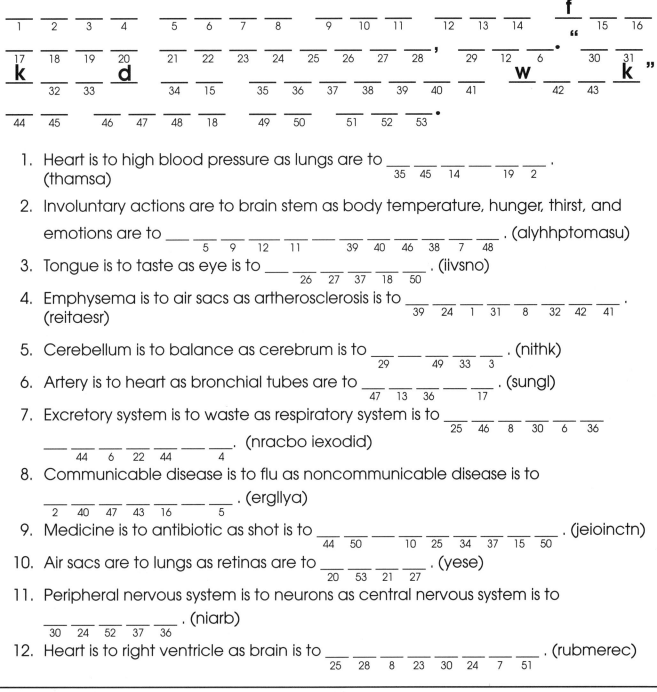

```
__  __  __  __   __  __  __  __   __  __  __   __  __  __  f   __  __
 1   2   3   4    5   6   7   8    9  10  11   12  13  14     15  16

__  __  __  __   __  __  __  __  __  __  __   __  12   6  •   __  __  "
17  18  19  20   21  22  23  24  25  26  27  28   29          30  31
 k       d                                              w        k
   __  __     __  __   __  __  __  __  __  __  __  __       __  __
   32  33     34  15   35  36  37  38  39  40  41           42  43

__  __   __  __   __  __   __  __  __  •
44  45   46  47   48  18   49  50   51  52  53
```

1. Heart is to high blood pressure as lungs are to __ __ __ __ __ .
   (thamsa)   35 45 14 19 2

2. Involuntary actions are to brain stem as body temperature, hunger, thirst, and
   emotions are to __ __ __ __ __ __ __ __ __ __ __ . (alyhhptomasu)
                     5 9 12 11   39 40 46 38 7 48

3. Tongue is to taste as eye is to __ __ __ __ __ . (iivsno)
                                    26 27 37 18 50

4. Emphysema is to air sacs as artherosclerosis is to __ __ __ __ __ __ __ __ .
   (reitaesr)   39 24 1 31 8 32 42 41

5. Cerebellum is to balance as cerebrum is to __ __ __ __ __ . (nithk)
                                               29   49 33 3

6. Artery is to heart as bronchial tubes are to __ __ __ __ __ . (sungl)
                                                 47 13 36   17

7. Excretory system is to waste as respiratory system is to __ __ __ __ __ __
                                                             25 46 8 30 6 36
   __ __ __ __ __ . (nracbo iexodid)
   44 6 22 44   4

8. Communicable disease is to flu as noncommunicable disease is to
   __ __ __ __ __ __ __ . (ergllya)
    2 40 47 43 16   5

9. Medicine is to antibiotic as shot is to __ __ __ __ __ __ __ __ __ . (jeioinctn)
                                            44 50   10 25 34 37 15 50

10. Air sacs are to lungs as retinas are to __ __ __ __ . (yese)
                                             20 53 21 27

11. Peripheral nervous system is to neurons as central nervous system is to
    __ __ __ __ __ . (niarb)
    30 24 52 37 36

12. Heart is to right ventricle as brain is to __ __ __ __ __ __ __ __ . (rubmerec)
                                                25 28 8 23 30 24 7 51
```
```

Name _____

National Little League Baseball Week

Let's Play Ball!

Boys and girls all across America benefit from the Little League baseball organization. It provides them with opportunities to develop athletic, teamwork, and social skills. National Little League Baseball Week is the second week in June.

Another important part of American culture was founded on June 16, 1903. To discover what it is, write the answer to each clue in the puzzle. Then, write the outside letters on the blanks in numerical order.

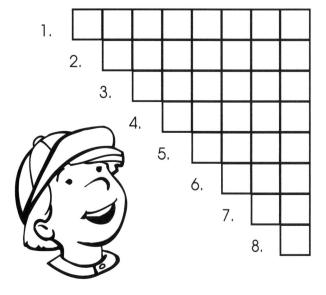

1.
2.
3.
4.
5.
6.
7.
8.

16.
15.
14.
13.
12.
11.
10.
9.

— — — — — — — — — —   — — — — — — — — — —

1. closely acquainted; well known

2. not paid in time; delinquent

3. to begin again; continue

4. thick

5. a friend or companion

6. homophone for *won*

7. homophone for *two*

8. fourth vowel in the alphabet

9. 18th letter of the alphabet

10. abbreviation for a system that cools air in cars and homes

11. homophone for *to*

12. homophone for *seem*

13. a hook or catch for holding two things together

14. a condition in which the blood is low in red blood cells

15. line where the sky seems to meet the earth

16. usual; regular; normal

Name _____

Super U.S. Symbols

The Continental Congress adopted the United States' flag on June 14, 1777. This is known as Flag Day.

Congress adopted the design for another important American symbol on June 20, 1782. To find out what the symbol is, write the answer for each clue on the blanks. Each answer will begin with the prefix *con-*, as in *Congress*, or *com-*, as in *combine*. Both prefixes mean *with* or *together*. Then, write the shaded letters on the blanks.

1. to make hard to understand ___ ___ ___ ___ ___ ___ ___ ___ | ___

2. including all or most of the details ___ ___ ___ ___ ___ ___ ___ | ___ ___ ___ ___ ___

3. to mix up in the mind ___ ___ ___ ___ ___ ___ ___ |

4. a group of people meeting for a religious service ___ ___ ___ ___ ___ ___ | ___ ___ ___ ___

5. to look at two things to see how they are the same or different ___ ___ ___ ___ ___ ___ | ___

6. a meeting of people to discuss something ___ ___ ___ ___ ___ ___ | ___ ___ ___ ___

7. to exchange information ___ ___ ___ ___ ___ ___ ___ ___ | ___ ___ ___

8. to take part in a contest ___ ___ ___ ___ ___ | ___ ___

9. money given to a person for making a sale ___ ___ ___ ___ ___ ___ | ___ ___ ___ ___

10. to focus intently on one issue ___ ___ ___ ___ | ___ ___ ___ ___ ___ ___

11. a plot; a secret plan to do something bad ___ ___ ___ ___ ___ ___ | ___ ___

12. to bring to an end ___ ___ ___ ___ | ___ ___ ___ ___

___ ___ ___ ___ ___ ___ ___ ___ ___ ___ ___ ___ **of the United States**

Name _____

A Day for Dad

Father's Day is observed on the third Sunday of June. It honors dads and is a great time to express gratitude and appreciation for your father.

Use each clue to write a word in the boxes. Each word contains letters from the word *appreciation.*

1. heavy fabric that covers floors

2. attention; heed

3. become visible

4. a fixed share or portion

5. a box or other container usually made of cardboard or plastic

6. a mom or dad

7. to walk or strut in a spirited manner

8. to keep or hold

9. the inner layer of the lining of the eyeball

10. to have to do with

11. words that describe a picture in a book, magazine, or newspaper

12. to choose for an office or position

13. a fruit that looks like a small peach

14. without any doubt

15. an action in return for another action

Name _____

Mmmm . . . Milk!

June is Dairy Month. What a great time to enjoy the great taste of milk and the many products made from it!

Write an answer in the boxes for each clue. Then, write the shaded letters in order to spell the name of some delicious dairy treats. Hint: All answers end in the suffix *-ive*.

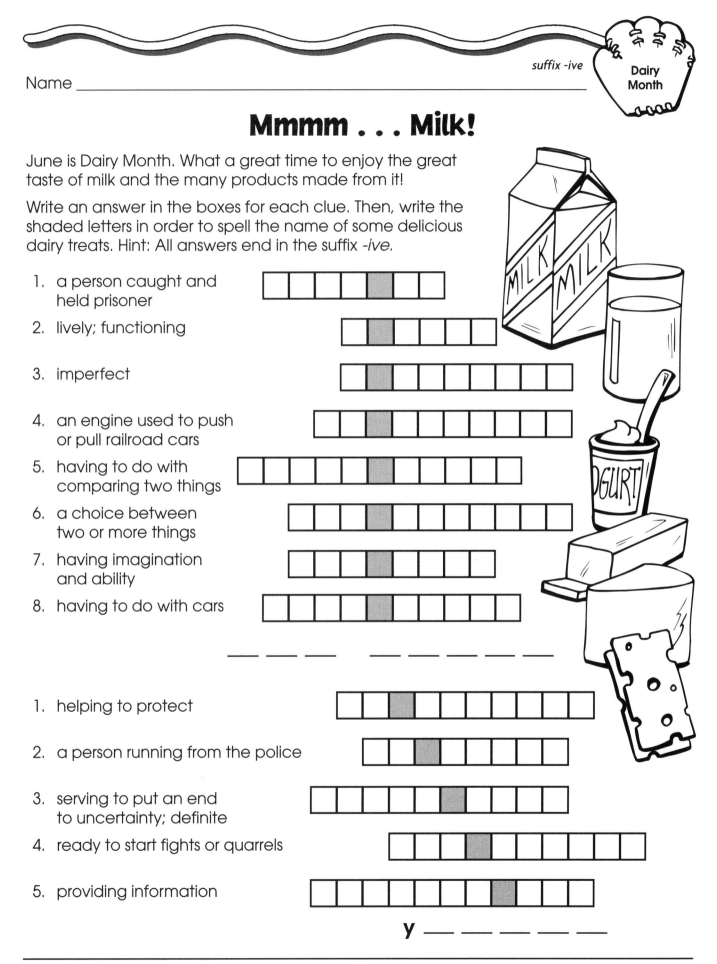

1. a person caught and held prisoner

2. lively; functioning

3. imperfect

4. an engine used to push or pull railroad cars

5. having to do with comparing two things

6. a choice between two or more things

7. having imagination and ability

8. having to do with cars

____ ____ ____ ____ ____ ____ ____ ____

1. helping to protect

2. a person running from the police

3. serving to put an end to uncertainty; definite

4. ready to start fights or quarrels

5. providing information

y ____ ____ ____ ____ ____

American Rivers Month

Name _____

Wonderful Water

American Rivers Month is celebrated in June. This is a great time to get out and appreciate the natural beauty provided by our country's rivers.

Complete the puzzle using the names of American rivers or words pertaining to them.

Across

4. second longest U.S. river
7. helped create the Grand Canyon
8. famous for its Niagara Falls
11. starting point of a river; can be a melting glacier or an overflowing lake
12. a triangular piece of land at the mouth of a large river

Down

1. longest U.S. river
2. at its mouth lies the harbor of New York City
3. Spanish for "large river"; forms part of U.S./Mexico boundary
5. links the Great Lakes and the Atlantic Ocean
6. all of the brooks and streams that carry water to a river
9. part of a river where water moves quickly over large rocks
10. forms boundary between Maryland, West Virginia, and Virginia

Name _____

Fabulously Fresh

June is National Fresh Fruit and Vegetable Month. This is the perfect time to enjoy all of these fresh, healthy foods. They taste great eaten alone or when used as ingredients in special dishes.

Ingredient contains the prefix *in-*. Use the clues below to write words beginning with the prefixes *in-* or *im-*. Then, use the number code to complete the puzzle to learn about one incredible piece of fruit.

1. to plunge or dip, especially into a fluid ___ ___ ___ ___ ___ ___ ___
   <small>11 6 6 4 5 22 17</small>

2. to affect or alter ___ ___ ___ ___ ___ ___ ___ ___ ___
   <small>11 12 29 8 25 4 10 28 4</small>

3. a natural aptitude ___ ___ ___ ___ ___ ___ ___ ___
   <small>11 15 18 3 11 10 28 3</small>

4. to create or produce for the first time ___ ___ ___ ___ ___ ___
   <small>11 12 27 21 15 13</small>

5. to establish or apply by authority ___ ___ ___ ___ ___ ___
   <small>11 6 24 9 19 20</small>

6. to contaminate with disease ___ ___ ___ ___ ___ ___
   <small>11 12 29 14 28 3</small>

7. to bring as merchandise into a place or country ___ ___ ___ ___ ___ ___
   <small>11 6 24 9 5 13</small>

8. to set in from the margin ___ ___ ___ ___ ___ ___
   <small>11 12 26 7 16 13</small>

9. to exert an enlivening or exalting influence upon ___ ___ ___ ___ ___ ___ ___
   <small>11 10 18 24 11 5 7</small>

10. to teach ___ ___ ___ ___ ___ ___ ___ ___
    <small>11 12 18 13 5 25 28 13</small>

11. to draw in as a participant ___ ___ ___ ___ ___ ___ ___
    <small>11 12 27 9 8 27 7</small>

12. to live or dwell in ___ ___ ___ ___ **b** ___ ___
    <small>11 10 23 1 11 3</small>

13. virtue of honesty and morality ___ ___ ___ ___ ___ ___ ___ ___
    <small>11 12 3 4 22 5 11 13</small>

14. to swell with air or gas ___ ___ ___ ___ ___ ___ ___
    <small>11 12 29 8 2 13 21</small>

1	w	2	3	4	5	6	7	8	9	10		11	12		13	14	15	16	17	18	19	20	21
22	5	4	w		3	9	w	7	11	22	23		2	6	0		24	9	25	10	26	18	!
11	3		24	5	9	27	11	26	7	26		22	20	16	21	5	9	25	18				
19	8	11	28	7	19		29	9	5		6	9	5	4		13	23	2	10		5	0	0
	24	7	9	24	8	4	!																

Word Games: Grades 5–6

Name _____

An Amazing Lady

Helen Keller overcame serious physical handicaps. Unable to hear, see, or speak after an illness at age two, Keller went on to do great things with the help of Annie Sullivan and others.

Helen Keller is recognized as both an author and lecturer. Use the letters in these words as clues to find the two two-letter pairs to complete each word. Each letter pair can be used only once.

ug	or	ge	ch	ft	nt	rn
ta	ri	er	ri	ct	um	sy
le	tt	ng	od	ll	ro	in
el	ht	nc	ya	de	ar	ce

1. v o   a
2. f o   u
3. m u   t
4. a n   h
5. n o   o
6. s t   r
7. c o   l
8. a c   e
9. c a   c
10. r e   t
11. c l   u
12. s t   r
13. m o   e
14. t h   r

Name _____

Reasons for the Seasons

If you live in the northern hemisphere, the longest day of the year is either June 21 or 22. This is when the summer solstice occurs. Solstice is a point in the Earth's orbit around the sun where the amount of daylight is either the longest or the shortest.

Two times a year, an equinox takes place. To find out what this is, write the answer in the puzzle for each clue. Then, write the first letter of each line on the blanks.

Equinox is when the sun is __ __ __ __ __ __ __ __   __ __ __ __ __

__ __ __   __ __ __ __ __ __ __ **, and the hours of daylight and night are equal.**

_____ (1) __
_____ (2) __ __
_____ (3) __ __ __
_____ (4) __ __ __ __
_____ (5) __ __ __ __ __
_____ (6) __ __ __ __ __ __
_____ (7) __ __ __ __ __ __ __
_____ (8) __ __ __ __ __ __
_____ (9) __ __ __ __ __
_____ (10) __ __ __ __
_____ (11) __ __ __
_____ (12) __

1. __
2. __ __
3. __ __ __
4. __ __ __ __
5. __ __ __ __ __
6. __ __ __ __ __ __
7. __ __ __ __ __ __ __
8. __ __ __ __ __ __
9. __ __ __ __ __
10. __ __ __
11. __ __
12. ▲

1. fourth letter of the alphabet
2. abbreviation for *identification*
3. not cooked
4. a sound that is heard again when sound waves bounce back from a surface
5. a movement that many people are interested in; a reason
6. to go from one place to another
7. a liquid used to soften skin
8. a large boat
9. dry and barren
10. part of a sea that cuts into a coastline to form a hollow curve
11. abbreviation for Ohio
12. 22nd letter of the alphabet

1. second vowel in the alphabet
2. abbreviation for Texas
3. a plain little house or cabin
4. something other than
5. to keep away from by careful planning
6. to drink; satisfy
7. needing quick action
8. terrible
9. homophone for *team*
10. strange; peculiar
11. abbreviation for Rhode Island

First
National
Park

Name _____

Perfect Parks

During June and the other summer months, many people take advantage of some of the spectacular national parks that exist in the U.S. Do you know which park was the country's first national park? It was established in 1872.

To find out the name, read the phonetic patterns and write the names of the national parks below. Unscramble the words to learn in which state each park is located. The letters in the shaded boxes will spell the name of the first national park.

__ __ __ __ __ __ __ __ __ __ __ __ __ __ __ __

1. yō-'se-mə-tē ☐☐☐☐☐☐☐☐ rainofclai _____

2. 'grand'tē-,tän ☐☐☐☐☐ ☐☐☐☐ wingyom _____

3. ,bad-,land'es ☐☐☐☐☐☐☐ hotsu tadako _____

4. 'e-vər-,glādz ☐☐☐☐☐☐☐☐☐ raidofl _____

5. si-'kwȯi-ə ☐☐☐☐☐☐ clnofiaria _____

6. 'red-ˌwu̇d ☐☐☐☐☐☐ wingyom _____

7. 'pe-trə-ˌfīd 'fȯr-əst ☐☐☐☐☐☐☐☐
☐☐☐☐☐ roanzia _____

8. 'ma-məth 'kāv ☐☐☐☐☐☐
☐☐☐☐ cukentyk _____

9. 'zī-ən ☐☐☐☐ haut _____

10. 'brīs 'kan-yən ☐☐☐☐☐
☐☐☐☐☐ tauh _____

11. 'mau̇nt rə-'nir ☐☐☐☐☐
☐☐☐☐☐☐ nosinghawt _____

Name _____

A Coveted Award

Thurgood Marshall was the first African-American associate justice of the Supreme Court. He was born on July 2, 1908. Marshall was also the recipient of a famous award given to African-Americans who reach the highest achievements in their fields.

To find out the name of this award, write the answer in the boxes for each clue. Each answer will go one letter past the next number. This is because each new word begins with the last two letters of the word before it. Then, write the shaded letters in Roman numeral order on the blanks.

___ ___ ___ ___ ___ ___ ___ ___   ___ ___ **d** ___ ___
 I   II III IV   V   VI VII VIII   IX   X   XI XII

1. like a suburb
2. agony; sorrow
3. to cover with something that protects
4. physical fitness of body and mind
5. for this or that reason
6. to move in a circle around something
7. a large ship or boat
8. to get rid of
9. not fully worked out or final; preliminary
10. plant life
11. spectator
12. to throw forth lava, water, gases, or other materials

Quebec Founded

Our North American Neighbor

Samuel de Champlain, a French explorer, founded the Canadian city of Quebec on July 3, 1608. About 25 percent of Canada's people live in Quebec, the largest in area of Canada's 10 provinces.

Circle the words relating to Canada in the puzzle. Words appear horizontally, vertically, and diagonally. Then, write the uncircled letters in order to learn more about Canada.

```
C D L E I H S N A I D A N A C O
B A P P A L A C H I A N E A N N
A R R D A N S N O R T H W E S T
I S I S T O K Q H E S E F C O A
N D N T L V A U A R G E O Y N R
S T C L I A T E C O U N U U T I
R Y E A I S C B N T H E N K W O
O R E W L C H E D I N A D O A R
E A D R I O E C T C V O L N N T
A I W E N T W S O U P R A O V I
N C A N E I A S T L A N N D T E
R R R C I A N T O R U I D E S S
X W D E A B O T I N A M R O S T
D E P M K C I W S N U R B W E N
E X O P R Z L M G P R D S I L E
G E A D E L S T A T R E B L A Z
```

British Columbia	Ontario	New Brunswick	Nunavut
Alberta	Quebec	Prince Edward	Appalachian
Saskatchewan	Newfoundland	Northwest	St. Lawrence
Manitoba	Nova Scotia	Yukon	Canadian Shield

— — — — — — — — — — — — — — — — — — —

— — — — — — — — — — — — — — — — —

— — — — — — — — — — **10** — — — — — — — — . — —

— — **3** — — — — — — — — — — — — — .

Independence Day

Name _____

Happy 4th of July!

The 4th of July is a fun holiday celebrated all across America. It commemorates the adoption of the Declaration of Independence by the Continental Congress on July 4, 1776.

Circle the words relating to this holiday in the puzzle. Words appear horizontally, vertically, and diagonally. Then, write the uncircled letters in order on the blanks to learn the names of the five men who met together to draw up this famous document.

Great Britain	independence	declaration	freedom	delegates
red, white, and blue	terminate	ancestor	colonies	Congress
parliament	union	states	fireworks	celebration

1. _ _ _ _ _ _ _   _ _ _ _ _ _ _ _ _

2. _ _ _ _   _ _ _ _ _

3. _ _ _ _   _ _ _ _ _ _ _ _ _

4. _ _ _ _ _ _ _   _ . _ _ _ _ _ _ _ _ _ _ _

5. _ _ _ _ _ _   _ _ _ _ _ _ _

t	f	i	r	e	w	o	r	k	s	h	o	m	a	p
s	c	o	n	g	r	e	s	s	j	e	f	f	e	a
r	s	o	n	d	c	j	o	h	n	a	d	n	c	r
s	r	o	t	s	e	c	n	a	a	m	n	o	s	l
t	b	e	e	n	l	p	f	r	a	o	l	i	n	i
a	k	l	r	i	e	n	e	r	i	o	o	t	b	a
t	d	e	m	r	b	t	r	n	n	l	i	a	v	m
e	e	i	i	n	r	g	u	i	d	s	t	r	o	e
s	l	n	n	r	a	o	e	g	e	e	r	a	s	n
h	e	e	a	r	t	s	m	a	n	r	n	l	o	t
p	g	h	t	s	i	t	r	o	l	x	c	c	m	g
r	a	s	e	b	o	r	x	m	d	l	o	e	e	z
d	t	m	e	c	n	g	e	f	r	e	e	d	o	m
r	e	d	w	h	i	t	e	a	n	d	b	l	u	e
t	s	n	i	a	t	i	r	b	t	a	e	r	g	f

Name _____

A Wonderful Waterway

The Erie Canal was the first important national waterway to be built in the U.S. Work began on this project on July 4, 1817. Its completion helped New York City develop into the important financial center of the U.S. that it is today.

To find out what the Erie Canal joins, write an answer for each clue on the blanks. Each answer begins with the prefix *super-* or *sub-*. Then, use the number code to complete the sentence below.

1. relating to a speed greater than the speed of sound

 __ __ __ __ __ __ __ __ __
 18   17 10 6 3 20 4 33

2. to receive a periodical or service regularly

 __ __ __ __ __ __ __ __ __
 6   18 33 10 1   11

3. less than total

 __ __ __ __ __ __ __
 6   2 32 13 12 26

4. to direct a group of people

 __ __ __ __ __ __ __ __
 18   11 10   30 6 8

5. above average quality

 __ __ __ __ __ __ __
 6   34 10 1 3 10

6. like a suburb

 __ __ __ __ __ __ __
 6   10   15 5

7. the utmost degree; exceptional

 __ __ __ __ __ __ __ __ __ __
 18   34 10 14 19 29 30

8. to get control over someone or something

 __ __ __ __ __ __
 18   21   17

9. an underground public transportation system

 __ __ __ __ __ __
 18   35

10. the act of subtracting one number from another

 __ __ __ __ __ __ __ __ __ __
 6   7 10 24 31 22 1   36

11. a large food store

 __ __ __ __ __ __ __ __ __ __
 18   17 10   27 10 16 23 2

12. following close after

 __ __ __ __ __ __ __ __ __
 18   18 11   34 28 25

13. to put, go, or stay underwater

 __ __ __ __ __ __ __
 6   23 10 9 11

 __ __ j __ __ __ __ h __ __ __ __ __
 1 2   3 4 5 6   7   8   9 10 11 12 13

 __ __ __ __ __ __ __ __ __h__ __
 14 15 16 17 18   19 20 21   22   23

 __ __ __ __ __ __ __ __ __ __ __ __ .
 24 25 26 27 28 29 30 31   32 33 34 35 36

Name _____

Circus Fun

P. T. Barnum helped found the most famous circus in history—the Ringling Brothers and Barnum & Bailey Circus. He was born on July 5, 1810.

Complete the crossword puzzle using words relating to the circus.

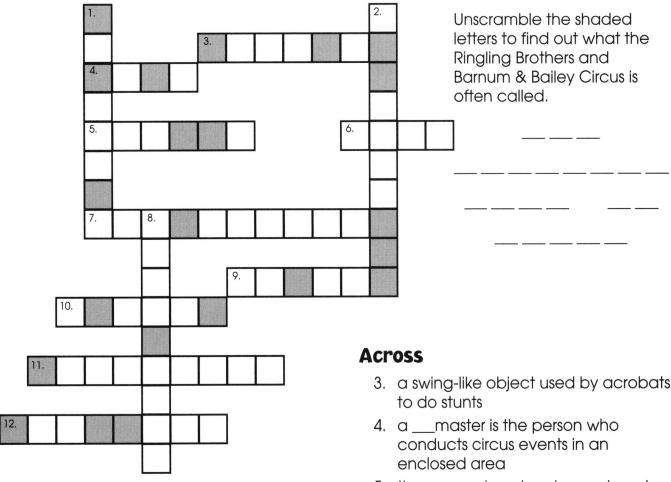

Unscramble the shaded letters to find out what the Ringling Brothers and Barnum & Bailey Circus is often called.

___ ___ ___

___ ___ ___ ___ ___ ___ ___

___ ___ ___ ___ ___

___ ___ ___ ___ ___

Across

3. a swing-like object used by acrobats to do stunts
4. a ___master is the person who conducts circus events in an enclosed area
5. the name given to a large circus tent
6. a group of musicians who play music at a circus
7. tumbling moves
9. people in costume who make people laugh
10. an event in which circus performers and animals march around
11. _____ riders ride on the backs of horses
12. a thin piece of wire on which tightrope walkers walk

Down

1. performers who do tumbling tricks
2. circus performers who do tricks in the air
8. where people can see the animals up close in their cages

Working for Women

The first women's rights convention in the U.S. met at Seneca Falls, New York, on July 19, 1848. Lucretia Mott and Elizabeth Cady Stanton worked diligently, along with many others, to help women gain the right to vote.

Mott and Stanton are to women's rights as Martin Luther King, Jr. is to African-Americans' rights. Complete each analogy. Then, use the number code to write the names of two other famous women suffragists.

1. Michael Jordan is to basketball as Mark McGwire is to ___ ___ ___ ___ ___ ___ ___ ___ .
   6 4 18 22 6 7 14 14

2. George W. Bush is to United States as Tony Blair is to ___ ___ ___   ___ ___ ___ ___ .
   22 7 9   6   9 4 21

3. Thomas Edison is to electric lamp as Eli Whitney is to ___ ___ ___ ___ ___   ___ ___ .
   20 19 9 11 8   12

4. Bill Clinton is to Al Gore as George W. Bush is to ___ ___ ___   ___ ___ ___ ___ ___ ___ .
   16   16 10 22 12 22 17

5. Michelangelo is to sculpture as Leonardo da Vinci is to ___ ___ ___ ___ ___ ___ ___ ___ .
   7 8 9 21

6. Lance Armstrong is to bicycles as Tony Hawk is to ___ ___ ___ ___ ___ ___ ___ ___ ___ ___ ___ ___ .
   18 7 19 22 6 11 4 1

7. Steven Spielberg is to motion pictures as Maya Angelou is to ___ ___ ___ ___ ___ ___ .
   11 22 9 17

8. Orville Wright is to pilot as John H. Glenn, Jr. is to ___ ___ ___ ___ ___ ___ ___ ___ ___ .
   4 1 9 20 5 7 15 19

9. Kristi Yamaguchi is to figure skating as Mia Hamm is to ___ ___ ___ ___ ___ ___ .
   3 20 16 16 22

10. Tiger Woods is to golf as Faith Hill is to ___ ___ ___ ___ .
    2 18 16

11. John F. Kennedy is to Jacqueline as Bill Clinton is to ___ ___ ___ ___ ___ ___ ___ .
    10 14 14 4 13

12. Bill Gates is to Microsoft as Walt Disney is to ___ ___ ___ ___ ___ ___ .
    3 8 22 17

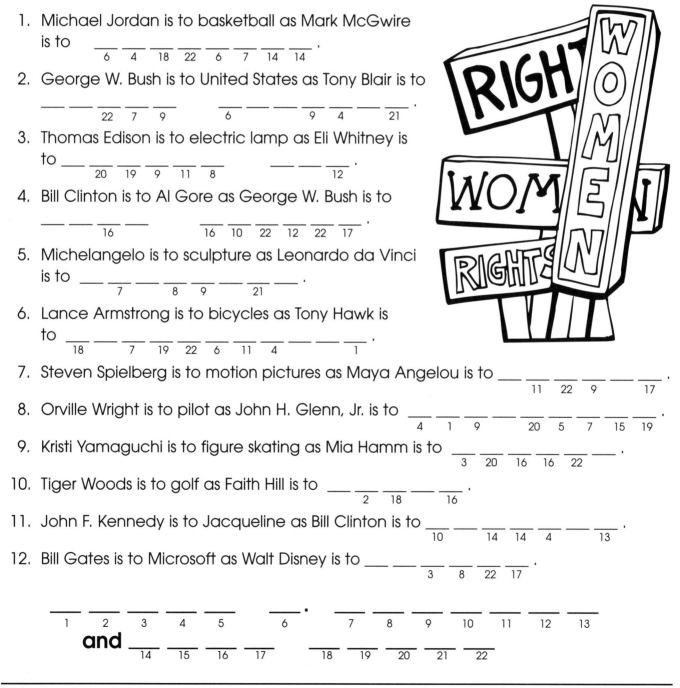

___ ___ ___ ___ ___   ___   ___ ___ ___ ___ ___ ___ ___ .
1 2 3 4 5   6   7 8 9 10 11 12 13

and ___ ___ ___ ___   ___ ___ ___ ___ ___ .
14 15 16 17   18 19 20 21 22

A Famous First

The week containing July 20 is Space Week. This week commemorates the anniversary of the first person walking on the moon. In 1969, the *Apollo 11* astronauts made the first landing on the moon. They landed on the Sea of Tranquility—a large, dark-colored lava plain.

To learn the name of the first man to walk on the moon, use the letters in *Sea of Tranquility* and the clues below to write a word in the boxes for each clue. Then, write the circled letters in order on the blanks.

1. a unit or group of four lines of verse

2. the answer to a division problem

3. delicate; fragile; not strong

4. not speaking; making no sound

5. free from dirt and germs

6. to soak completely through

7. not moving or not capable of being moved

8. something that is asked in order to find out information

9. able to reason; thinking clearly

10. a shape with four equal sides

11. living or being alone

12. to look with the eyes partly closed

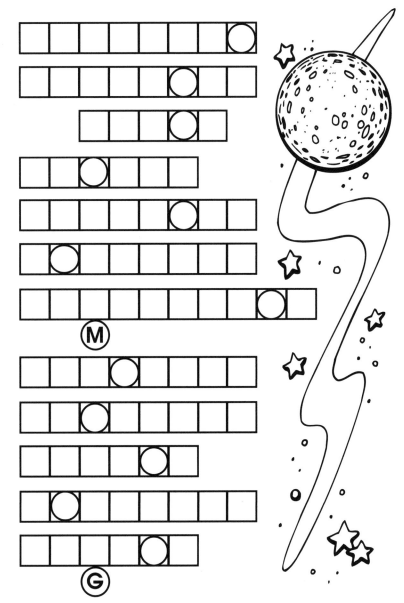

_____ __ __ __ __ __ __ __ . __ __ __ __ __ __ __ __ __

Name _____

vocabulary

Sweet, Cold, and Creamy

July is National Ice Cream Month. This is a great time to enjoy a bowl of your favorite flavor of ice cream!

Write an answer on the blanks for each clue. Then, use the number code to fill in the boxes with the names of three popular flavors of ice cream.

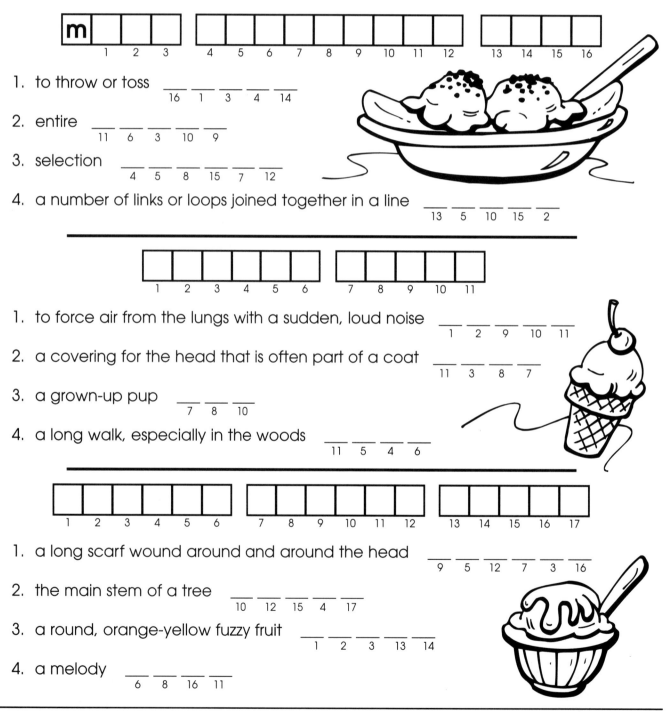

m ☐ ☐ ☐   ☐ ☐ ☐ ☐ ☐ ☐ ☐ ☐ ☐   ☐ ☐ ☐ ☐
1 2 3   4 5 6 7 8 9 10 11 12   13 14 15 16

1. to throw or toss ___ ___ ___ ___ ___
   16 1 3 4 14

2. entire ___ ___ ___ ___ ___
   11 6 3 10 9

3. selection ___ ___ ___ ___ ___ ___
   4 5 8 15 7 12

4. a number of links or loops joined together in a line ___ ___ ___ ___ ___
   13 5 10 15 2

☐ ☐ ☐ ☐ ☐ ☐   ☐ ☐ ☐ ☐ ☐
1 2 3 4 5 6   7 8 9 10 11

1. to force air from the lungs with a sudden, loud noise ___ ___ ___ ___ ___
   1 2 9 10 11

2. a covering for the head that is often part of a coat ___ ___ ___ ___
   11 3 8 7

3. a grown-up pup ___ ___ ___
   7 8 10

4. a long walk, especially in the woods ___ ___ ___ ___
   11 5 4 6

☐ ☐ ☐ ☐ ☐ ☐   ☐ ☐ ☐ ☐ ☐ ☐   ☐ ☐ ☐ ☐ ☐
1 2 3 4 5 6   7 8 9 10 11 12   13 14 15 16 17

1. a long scarf wound around and around the head ___ ___ ___ ___ ___ ___
   9 5 12 7 3 16

2. the main stem of a tree ___ ___ ___ ___ ___
   10 12 15 4 17

3. a round, orange-yellow fuzzy fruit ___ ___ ___ ___ ___
   1 2 3 13 14

4. a melody ___ ___ ___ ___
   6 8 16 11

Name _____

Explore Some More

Two famous explorers have birthdays in August. Meriwether Lewis was born on August 18, 1774, and William Clark was born on August 1, 1770. The expedition led by these two men extended from the Louisiana Territory to the Pacific coast.

Explorer includes the prefix *ex-*. This prefix can mean *out*, *from*, or *beyond*. Write a word with the prefix *ex-* for each clue.

1. to trade

2. to keep out or shut out

3. to release from an obligation

4. a large open area

5. a short trip taken for pleasure

6. a very skilled person

7. to stir up; arouse

8. to breathe out

9. to inspect

10. free from a usual rule or duty

11. to go beyond what is allowed

12. to think something will happen

13. outstanding

14. antonym of *interior*

15. not shared; sole

16. to put into words

17. correct and precise

18. to make clear or plain

19. to dig or dig out

20. species no longer existing

Name _____

First U.S. Census Began

Counting and Measuring

A census is an official counting to find out how many people there are in a particular area. It also determines people's ages, jobs, and other information. The first census in the United States began August 2, 1790.

Counting things is a way to measure them. Complete the crossword puzzle with a unit of measure as each answer.

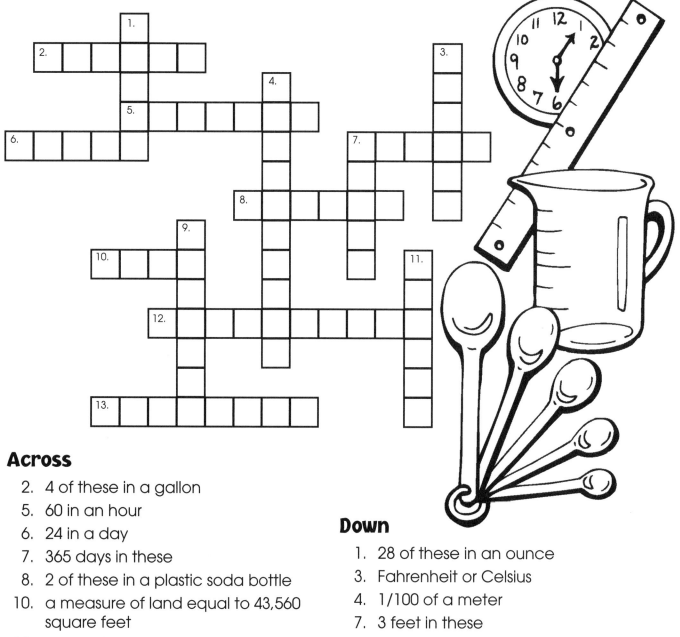

Across

2. 4 of these in a gallon
5. 60 in an hour
6. 24 in a day
7. 365 days in these
8. 2 of these in a plastic soda bottle
10. a measure of land equal to 43,560 square feet
12. equals 3 teaspoons
13. equals 1/3 of a tablespoon

Down

1. 28 of these in an ounce
3. Fahrenheit or Celsius
4. 1/100 of a meter
7. 3 feet in these
9. 10 in a century
11. 16 in a pound

Name _____

A Great Place to Visit

On August 10, 1846, the U.S. Congress established the Smithsonian Institution in Washington, D.C., a nonprofit corporation of scientific, educational, and cultural interests. Thousands of tourists visit this fascinating place each year.

Unscramble each word. The letters that spell Smithsonian Institution have been given as clues.

1.	roals	s				
2.	uidmh			m		
3.	saile		i			
4.	creat	t				
5.	herti		h			
6.	soloe				s	
7.	graco					o
8.	fento					n
9.	tliva		i			
10.	saiso		a			
11.	braun					n
12.	preig			i		
13.	cainb					n
14.	rents	s				
15.	latsl		t			
16.	fireb			i		
17.	tname					t
18.	urags		u			
19.	mocte					t
20.	sziee			i		
21.	cloor				o	
22.	neary					n

vocabulary **Phonograph Invented**

Invention Connection

On August 12, 1877, Thomas Edison invented the phonograph, or record player. This device ranks as one of the world's most original inventions. However, this was not the only thing Edison invented. To discover another Edison invention, write an answer in the boxes for each clue. Then, use the number code to complete the boxes at the right.

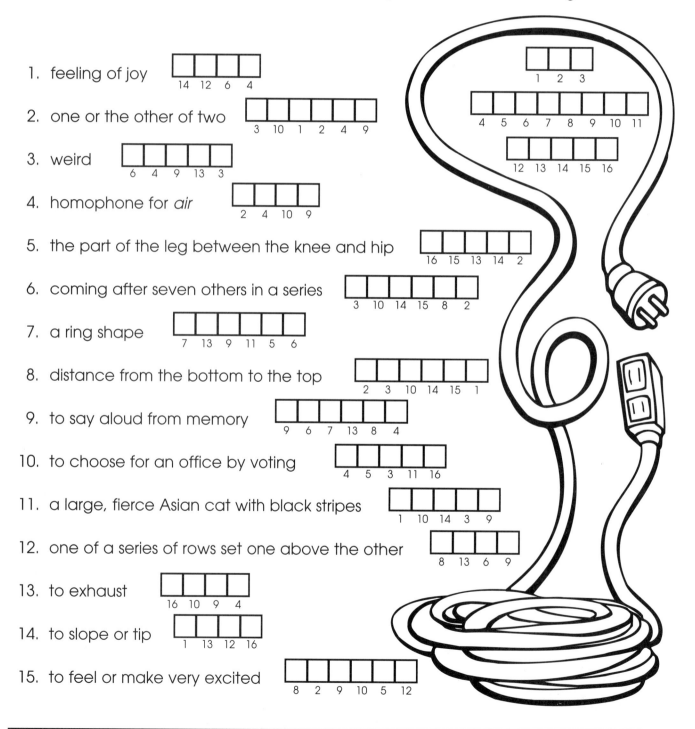

1. feeling of joy
   14 12 6 4

2. one or the other of two
   3 10 1 2 4 9

3. weird
   6 4 9 13 3

4. homophone for *air*
   2 4 10 9

5. the part of the leg between the knee and hip
   16 15 13 14 2

6. coming after seven others in a series
   3 10 14 15 8 2

7. a ring shape
   7 13 9 11 5 6

8. distance from the bottom to the top
   2 3 10 14 15 1

9. to say aloud from memory
   9 6 7 13 8 4

10. to choose for an office by voting
    4 5 3 11 16

11. a large, fierce Asian cat with black stripes
    1 10 14 3 9

12. one of a series of rows set one above the other
    8 13 6 9

13. to exhaust
    16 10 9 4

14. to slope or tip
    1 13 12 16

15. to feel or make very excited
    8 2 9 10 5 12

Top boxes codes:
1 2 3
4 5 6 7 8 9 10 11
12 13 14 15 16

Name _____

A Great Shortcut

The Panama Canal opened on August 15, 1914. This important waterway links the Atlantic and Pacific Oceans. It cuts about 8,000 miles off a ship's voyage from New York City to San Francisco.

Complete each word with two two-letter pairs. Each pair can be used only once. Use the letters in *the Panama Canal* as clues.

nw	va	ow	es	se	ct	ch
ca	er	ll	in	ay	ge	pe
tl	ap	gh	et	ts	ea	ta
un	an	ty	fe	uc	ve	mo

1. o u | | t | |
2. m i | | h | |
3. e f | | e | |
4. g r | | P | |
5. s a | | a | |
6. r u | | n | |
7. o b | | a | |
8. r e | | m | |
9. p l | | a | |
10. s a | | C | |
11. g r | | a | |
12. l a | | n | |
13. e s | | a | |
14. f o | | l | |

Orville Wright's Birthday

Right On, Wright Brothers!

Orville Wright and his brother, Wilbur, invented and built the first successful airplane. Orville was born on August 19, 1871.

To learn something else incredible these two brothers did, circle the aviation-related words in the puzzle. Then, write the uncircled letters in order on the blanks.

— — — — _ — — — _ — — — _ — — — — — ,

— — — — — — — — — — — — — — — —

— — — — — — - — — — — — — , — — — — — — — -

— — — — - — — — — — — — — — — — .

aviation   airplane   airport   warplane
pilot   North Carolina   jumbo jet   airmail service
Kitty Hawk   airliner   helicopter   Concorde
air pressure   aircraft   fighter jet   transport plane

```
t h h e y t r o p r i a m a d
e e n a l p t r o p s n a r t
t l h e w o e n a l p r a w r
k i t t y h a w k l a n d s f
i c e r t s t f l i i g h a a
t o d i e n a p o l r w e i i
r p r d j r i v o e c n e r r
a t o h r e a r v i r n e l p
v e c r e t a h a n a a i i r
i r n r t c m a c l f h l n e
a i o n h e l m p x t o r e s
t x c t g g o r s x t m o r s
i e r p i a i l a k d i j e u
o o p c f a j u m b o j e t r
n a i r m a i l s e r v i c e
```

A Famous Name

On August 24, 1814, British troops captured Washington, D.C. They did something that eventually gave an important landmark its name.

To find out what the troops did, write an answer in the puzzle for each clue. Then, write the outside letters in numerical order on the blanks.

They ___ ___ ___ ___ ___ ___   ___ ___ ___   ___ ___ ___ ___ ___   ___ ___ ___ ___ ___ .
    1 2 3 4 5 6   7 8 9   10 11 12 13 14   15 16 17 18 19

It was painted white to hide the scorch marks.

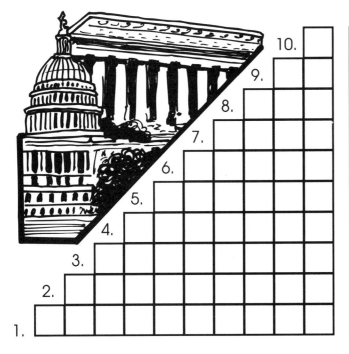
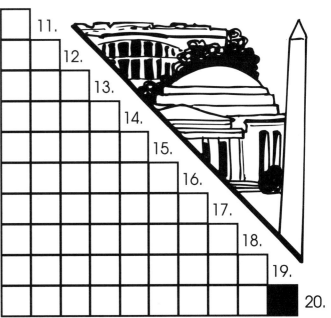

1. being of use; of great benefit
2. in complete agreement
3. to be like or similar to
4. not one or the other
5. to come into view; to appear
6. to live or reside; to keep thinking about
7. not false
8. not him
9. abbreviation for *each*
10. 23rd letter of the alphabet
11. eighth letter of the alphabet
12. third note of a musical scale
13. the hard stone in the center of a peach
14. a dull, steady pain
15. to sit on a tree limb
16. rhymes with *potato*
17. another word for *reindeer*
18. a large number; very many
19. to increase or strengthen
20. able to catch fire easily

Name _____

Women's Turn

August 26 is Women's Equality Day. Americans can celebrate the passing of the 19th Amendment on this day in 1920. To find out what the 19th Amendment called for, write an answer in the boxes for each clue. Then, write the letters in the shaded boxes in order on the blanks.

— — ____ ____ ____ — — — — — —

— — ____ ____ — .

1. genuine; real
2. a 3-beat dance for couples
3. past tense of *catch*
4. showing too much pride while looking down on others
5. a room to keep money safe in a bank
6. past tense of a verb that tells what you do when you are sleepy
7. clumsy
8. someone who writes books
9. synonym for *fall* (the season)
10. a small, shallow dish
11. not nice
12. female offspring
13. a metal, canvas, or wood covering that is fixed to a window or door frame
14. to stop
15. stretched tight
16. really terrific
17. having to do with automobiles
18. an opportunity for a singer or actor to be tested for a job
19. fine bits of wood that are produced when a saw cuts through wood
20. set off a rocket

Vocabulary List

The following is a partial list of the vocabulary students will use while completing the word games in this book. It was generated from fifth- and sixth- grade reading lists, as well as textbooks. Learning and understanding these words will help students achieve greater success in all academic areas.

abandon	athlete	chuckle	desperate	extensive
abbreviation	atrium	cinquain	dessert	extinguish
absurd	attempt	circumference	destructive	extraordinary
abundant	audition	citizen	development	extremely
accommodate	authentic	collective	difficult	fabulous
accomplishment	avalanche	column	digestion	Fahrenheit
accurate	avoidance	commander	disconnect	faith
achievement	awesome	communicable	discussion	familiar
acquaintance	awning	compliment	disease	fatigue
acrobat	basement	comprehensive	dividend	feast
agenda	beneficial	conclusive	document	festival
aggressive	binoculars	condemn	donate	fiery
agreement	biscuit	congregation	economics	flammable
ajar	bizarre	conjunction	economy	foreign
algebra	braille	consequence	edible	formality
allowable	brochure	consonant	educational	fracture
alternative	bronchial	continental	eerie	fragment
although	browse	continuous	effective	fragmentation
aluminum	burden	controversial	elaborate	frequently
amendments	burglar	convenience	elliptical	galaxy
analogous	calculator	cooperation	embarrass	geometry
analogy	candelabrum	corporation	emerge	glacier
ancestor	capacity	corral	enchantment	gnarled
anchor	caption	courteous	encourage	governor
anguish	caribou	coyotes	encouragement	grammar
announcement	carriage	creativity	enduring	hallucination
annually	categorize	crocodile	enormous	haughty
antennae	category	cultural	enough	hearth
antibiotic	caution	currency	equally	height
antonym	Celsius	daughter	equinox	helicopter
appearance	centimeter	decade	equipment	hesitant
applaud	centipede	decision	equivalent	homograph
artery	century	declaration	essay	homophone
ascend	cerebellum	decoding	ethnic	horizontal
asphalt	cerebrum	defiance	eventually	hostility
assertive	challenger	definition	evident	humidity
assign	characteristic	delicacy	excavate	humorous
asteroid	chemistry	delicious	exceptional	hyphen
astonish	chlorophyll	democrat	exclusive	ignorance
astronomical	chronological	denominator	excursion	illiterate
astronomy	chrysanthemum	depression	exploration	illusion

Vocabulary List (continued)

imaginary	nasal	postscript	seizure	taught
immerge	nationality	precipitation	seldom	technique
immigrant	naughty	predicate	selection	terrain
incorrect	necessary	preliminary	sensitive	theory
independence	neither	premature	separate	thesaurus
industrious	nephew	preposition	shampoo	thrifty
inferior	neutral	preserve	shoulder	tolerant
inflatable	neutrality	principle	significant	tourist
initiate	nuisance	privilege	silence	tradition
inspiring	numerator	proclamation	similar	tragedy
instinct	numerical	profession	solemn	tranquility
instruction	oasis	profit	solitary	transatlantic
integrity	obedient	progressive	somersault	transplant
intelligence	object	publisher	souvenir	trapeze
interruption	occasion	punctuation	spaghetti	trapezoid
irresponsible	occurrence	purpose	spectator	triumph
irreversible	opinion	quadruplet	splendor	unanimous
jaguars	orchestra	quarterback	squash	unforgettable
jeopardy	ordinary	quasar	squeeze	unicycle
journey	originate	quench	stampede	uniform
kayak	oxygen	quotation	stationary	unity
laboratory	parliament	quotient	stationery	universal
language	passenger	raccoons	steadfast	unusual
legend	passport	rationale	stethoscope	urban
legitimate	patented	ravenous	stomach	utensil
liberty	peculiar	reaction	strengthen	vacation
library	pennant	recommend	structure	valuable
luggage	penniless	recreation	stubborn	vascular
magnificent	perimeter	refreshment	submerge	ventricle
marvelous	periodical	reinforce	subscribe	versatile
mathematics	permanent	relativity	subsequent	vertical
meanness	permissible	remarkable	substantial	veteran
measurement	perpetual	republican	subtraction	villain
menorah	persecute	resemble	suburban	violent
meteoroid	persevere	resistance	successful	visualize
misbehave	phantom	respiratory	superior	vocabulary
misfortune	philosophical	reverent	superlative	volcanoes
misspell	phonetic	rhythm	supernova	wealthy
moccasin	pigeon	salvation	supersonic	weary
mosquitoes	plasma	sanitary	superstition	whether
movable	political	saturate	surrender	wrench
multiplication	popularity	schedule	survive	wrinkle
museum	possession	scientific	sweltering	yogurt
musician	posterity	seashore	synonym	

Vocabulary Enrichment Activities

The following activities provide a fun and challenging way to help students expand their vocabularies. These activities can be used as individual or group activities. Vocabulary development will help improve students' reading, writing, and testing skills.

Dictionary Decisions

Have students find new words and their definitions in a dictionary. Then, have students make up true and false statements about their words. In pairs, students can challenge each other with their statements. For example, one student might say, "A rock hound makes a good pet. True or false?" If the question is answered incorrectly, the student must use a dictionary to find the word's definition.

Puzzle Power

Challenge students to make their own word games to share with each other. Use the grids on pages 118 and 119 as guides. Ideas for using the grids are as follows:

Crossword Puzzle Grid—Have students use their spelling lists to make crossword puzzles. After the words are written in the puzzles, students can use clean grids to shade in the boxes that are not used. Then, students can number the puzzles and write definitions on the appropriate lines at the bottom of the page.

Word Search—Have students write the vocabulary words from specific subject areas in the grid. When all the words have been included, random letters can be added to fill the grids. List the words in the Word Bank. Exchange grids to solve.

Thesaurus Tunes

Have students write the words of their favorite songs or poems. Then, instruct students to use a thesaurus to write synonyms for as many words in the songs or poems as possible. Finally, have each student read the new song or poem to the rest of the class.

Word of the Day

Feature a word each day from the vocabulary list on pages 115 and 116. Encourage students to use the word either orally or in writing three times during the day. Challenge the students to find the word in written text. Keep track of how many times the word is found.

Word-Wide Web

The Word of the Day can also be studied by completing the Word-Wide Web on page 120. The web includes the word's definition, phonetic spelling, and origin. A synonym and antonym for the word should be included when possible, as well as a sentence using the word. Have students take turns completing the web for the daily featured word. Display the webs for review.

Name _____

Crossword Puzzle Grid

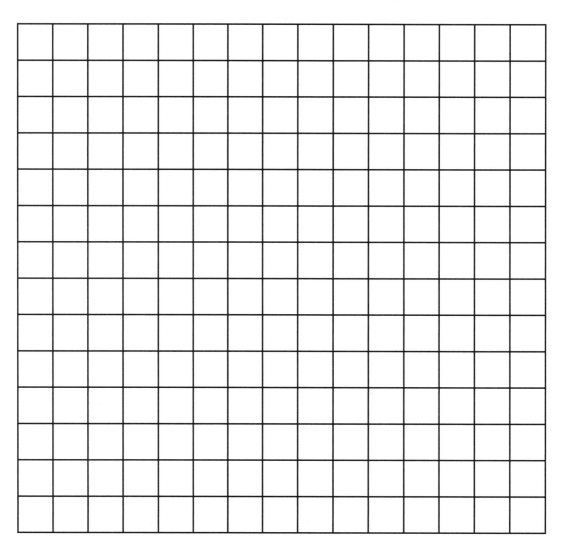

Across   **Down**

_____   _____

_____   _____

_____   _____

_____   _____

_____   _____

Name _____

Word Search Grid

Word Bank

Word-Wide Web

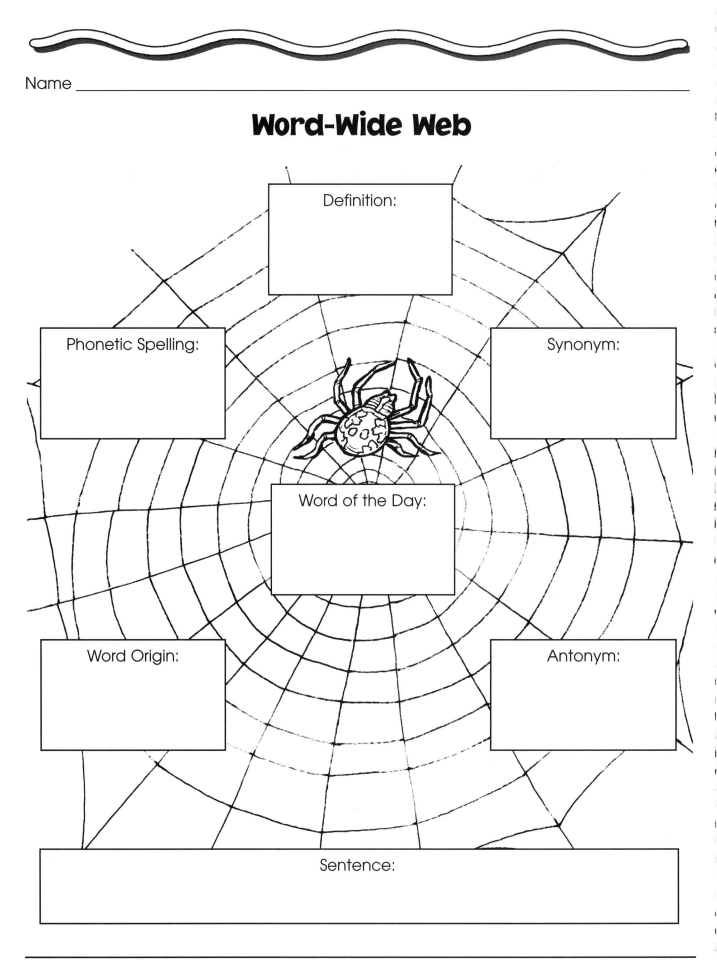

Definition:

Phonetic Spelling:

Synonym:

Word of the Day:

Word Origin:

Antonym:

Sentence:

Page 4

1. kneed or knead; 2. serial; 3. wood;
4. you; 5. groan; 6. altar; 7. brake;
8. guessed; 9. pour; 10. knows; New York
Sun; 11. chants; 12. fined; 13. urn;
14. ferry; 15. whole; 16. plane; 17. dear;
18. seller; 19. aloud; 20. chili or Chile;
21. bored; ten years old

Page 5

```
u                    s
  n o              A L
  i l l            n e w
  t o l d          d a r k
  e m p t y        c a n d y
d e m a n d        a s s i g n
  s t e e l        n a s a l
    t a s k        a j a r
    a n d          d i m
    t p            a m
    e
```

United States and Canada

Page 6

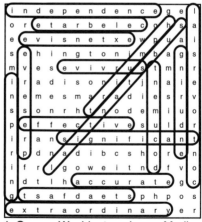

```
              f         p r o m i s e
              e         a
    s         r         t
  u         o b e d i e n t           h
  p     l   c         e               o
  p     o   i         n       p       s
  o     a   o         t o l e r a n t t
g r a t e f u l       o               i
  t     h   s         h   v           l
    e             h   p a r d o n     e
                  o   r   k
        a g g r e s s i v e
                  h
```

"The Star-Spangled Banner"

Page 7

1. a. friend; b. hearth; c. hinder; d. drain;
e. father; 2. a. claim; b. mail; c. lamb;
d. climb; 3. a. change; b. green; c. heel,
heal; d. hear, here
fifteen

Page 8

```
i n d e p e n d e n c e   g e l
o r e t a r b e l e c     h s a
e   e v i s n e t x e     w u a
s e h i n g t o n i   b a g s
m v e s e v i v r u s   t   i
i r a d i s o n i t j   n a r
n e m e s m a r r a d i e s u
s o n r h t n o d e m   i u o
p e f f e c t i v e   s u l l
i r a n s i g n i f i c a n t
r p d n a d i b c s h o r e n
i f r l g o w e i t n d f v o
n d t l h a c c u r a t e   g c
g t s a f d a e t s p h p o s
e x t r a o r d i n a r y e r
```

1. George Washington, James Madison;
2. James Madison; 3. Rhode Island

Page 9

Winter	Spring	Summer	Fall
Hanukkah	seedtime	watermelon	October
February	showers	August	November
snowflake	April	mosquitoes	Thanksgiving
Kwanzaa	sprout	independence	bonfires
blizzard	May	sweltering	autumn
Christmas	bloom	July	Halloween
frigid	windy	vacation	crisp
avalanche		fireworks	

Latin words for "equal" and "night."

Page 10

```
    e                  e
    m e                m e
    m e t              m e n
  m e a t            m e a n
s t e a m          n a m e s
  s e a t          s e a m
    s e t            s e a
    s e                e a
    e                  e
```

Page 11

e	x	p	e	n	s	i	v	e
i	n	f	e	r	i	o	r
i	n	n	o	c	e	n	t
f	o	l	l	o	w	e	r
c	r	o	o	k	e	d
o	r	d	i	n	a	r	y
w	o	r	t	h	l	e	s	s
g	e	n	e	r	o	u	s
p	e	r	m	a	n	e	n	t

j	o	l	l	y
l	i	q	u	i	d
h	e	a	v	y
e	a	r	l	y
r	o	u	g	h
s	p	e	n	d
r	a	r	e
n	o	i	s	y

John Chapman

Page 12

1. absurd; 2. crayon; 3. bounce; 4. victim;
5. street; 6. delays; 7. steaks; 8. lumber;
9. colony; 10. edible
Can I take you out?

Page 13

1. artery; 2. heart; 3. vein; 4. kidneys;
5. skull; 6. skin; 7. nerves; 8. brain;
9. skeleton; 10. tonsils; 11. plasma;
12. lungs; 13. liver; 14. muscles;
15. marrow
the equivalent of a small car

Page 14

1. exhale; 2. express; 3. extinct;
4. illiterate; 5. recall; 6. relocate;
7. unintelligent; 8. unusual; 9. inland;
10. incorrect; 11. prehistoric; 12. predict;
13. irresponsible; 14. irreversible;
15. irredeemable
Erie Canal opened to traffic

Page 15

Statue of
Liberty

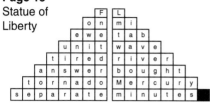

```
                    F   L
                  o n   m i
              e w e t   a b
          u n i t   w a v e
        t i r e d   r i v e r
    a n s w e r   b o u g h t
  t o r n a d o   M e r c u r y
s e p a r a t e   m i n u t e s ■
```

Page 16

```
  o                      o
  t o                    s o
  r o t                  s o n
  t r o t                n o s e
  o t t e r              s t o n e
  t o t e        o       n o t e
  t o t        o h       n o t
  o t        h o t       n o
  o        s h o t           o
         s h o o t
         h o o t
         t o o
         t o
         o
```

Page 17

-ness—state or quality of being;
-ous—full of, having the qualities of;
-able—able to be; capable of being;
-ly—like in appearance, manner, or
nature; having the characteristics of;
1. inflatable; 2. recognizable;
3. weariness; 4. happily; 5. wondrous;
6. equally; 7. fabulous; 8. poisonous;
9. continuous; 10. breakable;
11. enormous
Noah Webster

Page 18

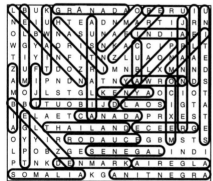

```
L B U K G R A N A D A O P E R U I U
N E F H T E A D M A R T I J R N
O L B W N A S U N A   I N D I A D
W I Y A O R I Z U N K A C C I P R L
T Z U F   T D O Z R I M N B L X M N D
Z A M   P N D N A T N Y A W R O N O S
A L L S T G L K E N Y A O C I T O A
B B I T U O B   J D L A O S I G T A
E L A E T C A N A D A P R X E S E S T
A G L T H A I L A N D E C E E R G E
O Y I R R O D A U C E G B M S T S
L P O B Z G E S E N E G A L I N D I
P T N K O D E N M A R K A I R E G L A
S O M A L I A K G A N I T N E G R A
```

Page 19

1. stubborn; 2. bubble; 3. accommodate;
4. occasion; 5. follow; 6. ballot; 7. difficult;
8. collar; 9. grammar; 10. common;
11. teammate; 12. waffles; 13. meddle;
14. parrot; 15. tomorrow; 16. carrots;
17. cassette; 18. scissors; 19. necessary;
20. tattle; 21. battle; 22. blizzard

Page 20

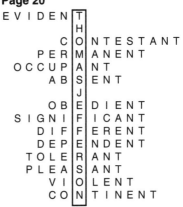

```
E V I D E N T
          H
      C   O N T E S T A N T
  P E R M A N E N T
          A
O C C U P A N T
          S
  A B S E N T
          J
      O B E D I E N T
S I G N I F I C A N T
  D I F F E R E N T
  D E P E N D E N T
  T O L E R A N T
  P L E A S A N T
      V I O L E N T
      C O N T I N E N T
```

Declaration of Independence

Page 21

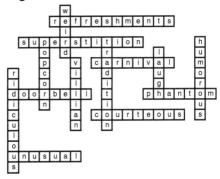

Page 22

```
h a l l u c i n a t i o n
l o c a t i o n
p r o m o t i o n
d i s c u s s i o n        Harding
d i r e c t i o n
n o t i o n
s u g g e s t i o n
```

```
d i g e s t i o n
c a u t i o n
r e s t r i c t i o n
d e f i n i t i o n        Garfield
p r o f e s s i o n
r e l a t i o n
s e l e c t i o n
d e p r e s s i o n
```

Page 23

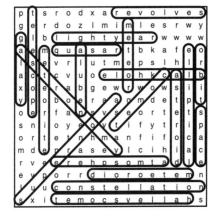

Page 24

1. termite; 2. meet; 3. omit; 4. totem;
5. trim; 6. tire; 7. rote; 8. time; 9. term;
10. tote; 11. star; 12. dirt; 13. stir; 14. tear;
15. ratio; 16. diet; 17. stare; 18. sod;
19. soar; 20. rose

Page 25

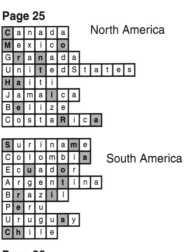

```
C a n a d a
M e x i c o
G r a n a d a              North America
U n i t e d S t a t e s
H a i t i
J a m a i c a
B e l i z e
C o s t a R i c a
```

```
S u r i n a m e
C o l o m b i a
E c u a d o r              South America
A r g e n t i n a
B r a z i l
P e r u
U r u g u a y
C h i l e
```

Page 26

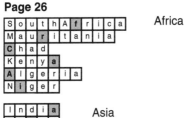

```
S o u t h A f r i c a       Africa
M a u r i t a n i a
C h a d
K e n y a
A l g e r i a
N i g e r
```

```
I n d i a                   Asia
C h i n a
J a p a n
L a o s
```

```
F r a n c e
A u s t r i a               Europe
S p a i n
G e r m a n y
N o r w a y
G r e e c e
```

Australia
Antarctica

Page 27

chocolate; sugar; pudding; fruit;
spaghetti; apple; yogurt; cereal; biscuit;
waffle; Answers may vary. Possible
answers include: 1. sugar; 2. waffle;
3. fruit; 4. biscuit; 5. cereal; 6. apple;
7. pudding; 8. chocolate; 9. yogurt;
10. spaghetti
potato chips

Page 28

```
t                 l
  h i           c o
  e n d         a c t
  g i f t       n o o n
r o d e o       s e i z e
e n o u g h     m u s e u m
a c c e p t     o b j e c t
  t h e i r     k a y a k
  a c h e       e a s t
  m u d         o u t
  e r           u s
  r             t
```

Page 29

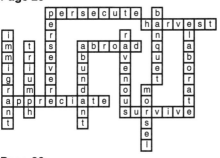

Page 30

disappear; dishonest; misspell;
misbehave; disagree; disloyal; mislead;
misprint; disconnect; disgrace; mistreat;
misfortune; discover; dismount; misplace;
disrobe

```
They filled paper and
cloth bags with hot
air to create hot air
balloons.
```

Page 31

yes; store; tour; cut
courtesy

point; less; spoil; steps
politeness

names; mess; man; mesa
meanness

Page 32

Tundra	Desert	Rain Forest	Savanna & Woodland	Temperate Forest
penguins	long, dry season	monkeys	giraffes	oak trees
extremely cold	dry	humid	hippos	raccoons
polar bears	Gila monsters	jaguars	elephants	elm trees
arctic foxes	oasis	palm trees	lions	squirrels
frozen subsoil	camels	wet	kangaroos	deer
	cacti	climbing vines	zebra	

Birds pick leftover food from their teeth.

Page 33

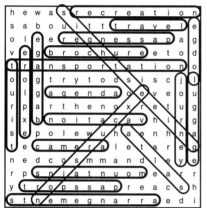

He was about to leave to try to discover the North Pole when he learned Commander Perry had just reached it.

Page 34

1. agreement; 2. enchantment;
3. development; 4. refreshment;
5. announcement; 6. settlement;
7. achievement; 8. measurement;
9. accomplishment; 10. equipment;
11. encouragement; 12. basement
The first human heart transplant

Page 35

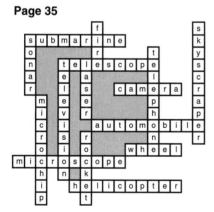

Page 36

1. Festival; 2. dreidel; 3. shammes;
4. dedication; 5. rabbi; 6. survived;
7. Judas Maccabee; 8. latkes;
9. tradition; 10. miracle; 11. nine;
12. gifts; 13. menorah; 14. temple;
15. gods

Page 37

4-letter words: 1. stir; 2. mass; 3. star;
4. miss; 5. math; 6. cram; 7. chat;
8. harm; 9. cash; 10. sham; 11. hair;
12. hiss; 13. this; 14. mist; 15. mast;
16. trim
5-letter words: 17. match; 18. charm;
19. smart; 20. scram; 21. chart; 22. shirt;
23. stair; 24. chair; 25. march; 26. trash
6-letter word: 27. starch

Page 38

1. unity; 2. self-determination; 3. collective work and responsibility; 4. cooperative economics; 5. purpose; 6. creativity;
7. faith
candle; feast; gifts

Page 39

The first ten amendments to the Constitution, called the Bill of Rights, were ratified. Today, Bill of Rights Day is celebrated on December 15.

Page 40

1. magnet; 2. cruise; 3. behave; 4. anchor;
5. biking; 6. palace; 7. barber; 8. praise;
9. solemn; 10. noodle; 11. wrench;
12. parent; 13. manage; 14. recent;
15. browse; 16. tissue; 17. lotion;
18. pardon; 19. rumble; 20. coward;
21. bridge; 22. breath; 23. struck;
24. hunger; 25. clover
roller skates

Page 41

Rosa Parks

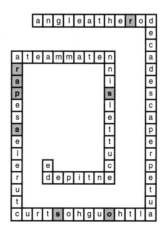

Page 42

```
        a                    a
      a t                  t a
    s a t                b a t
    s t a r              b e a t
    s t a r t            b e a s t
      t a r t            s e a t
        t a r              e a t
          r a                e a
            a                  a


        a                    a
      a s                  a b
    h a s                c a b
  c a s h              c r a b
c r a s h            b r a c e
  r a s h              r a c e
    r a h              c a r
      a h              C A
        a                    a
```

Page 43

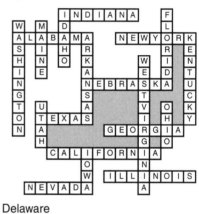

Delaware

Page 44

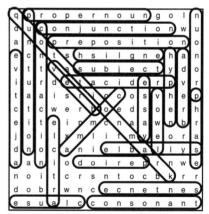

Page 45
1. permissible; 2. recommend;
3. pennant; 4. applaud; 5. otter;
6. hurricane; 7. stroller; 8. channel;
9. struggle; 10. innocent; 11. allowance;
12. antennae; 13. communicate;
14. flammable; 15. connect; 16. attempt;
17. immediately; 18. announce;
19. messenger; 20. alligator
concorde supersonic aircraft

Page 46
mathematics; republican; rapid;
quadruplet; shampoo; headache;
superhero; subtraction; century;
daughter; author; shiver; 1. republican;
2. quadruplet; 3. mathematics; 4. rapid;
5. superhero; 6. shampoo; 7. subtraction;
8. daughter; 9. author; 10. century;
11. shiver; 12. headache

Page 47

Page 48
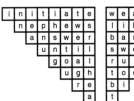

Inauguration Day

Page 49
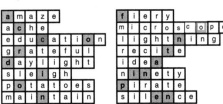

accordion; fountain pen

Page 50
cargo; usher; blend; asked; comet; brake;
boast; niece; salad; until; razor; rodeo;
gifts; stole; score; guilt; munch; parts;
rapid; vowel
"The Wizard of Menlo Park"

Page 51
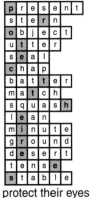

protect their eyes

Page 52
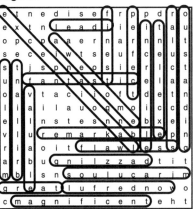

The Constitution sets no qualifications.
Justices are appointed by the president.

Page 53
1. raincoat; 2. handshake; 3. eyeball;
4. sweatshirt; 5. barefoot; 6. shortstop;
7. bedspread; 8. wristwatch;
9. needlepoint; 10. toothbrush;
11. sunglasses; 12. matchbox;
13. drawbridge; 14. chairman;
15. surfboard; 16. fingernail;
17. roadblock; 18. hairdresser

Page 54
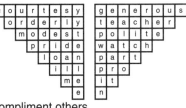

Page 55
1. James Monroe; 2. Franklin D.
Roosevelt; 3. William H. Harrison;
4. John Tyler; 5. James Buchanan;
6. Andrew Johnson; 7. Grover Cleveland;
8. James A. Garfield; 9. George W. Bush
T. Roosevelt

Page 56
athletes: 1. Williams; 2. Robinson;
3. Ashe
civil rights leaders: 4. King; 5. Parks;
6. Randolph
political figures: 7. Powell; 8. Chisholm;
9. Jordan

Page 57
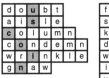

compliment others

Page 58
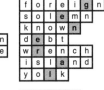

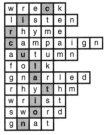

U.S. coin in general circulation

Page 59

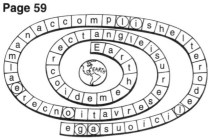

Galileo

Page 60

trustworthy; loyal; helpful; friendly;
courteous; kind; obedient; cheerful;
thrifty; brave; clean; reverent
be prepared; learning by doing

Page 61

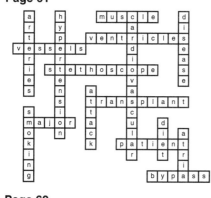

Page 62

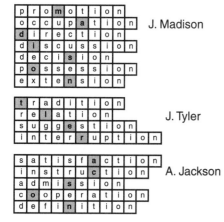

J. Madison

J. Tyler

A. Jackson

Page 63

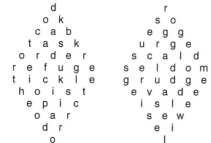

Doctor Theodor Seuss Geisel

Page 64

1. surrender; 2. accurate; 3. burglar;
4. calculator; 5. burden; 6. popular;
7. yogurt; 8. fracture; 9. alternate;
10. desperate; 11. cavern; 12. admiral
Francis Scott Key

Page 65

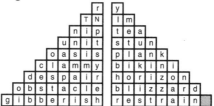

1. God; 2. country; 3. mankind

Page 66

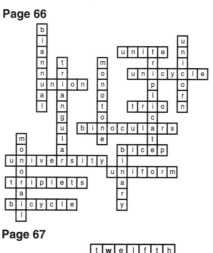

Page 67

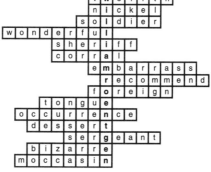

Page 68

Vegetables	Meat, Fish, nuts	Fruit	Breads, Rice, Pasta	Dairy
broccoli	pecans	strawberries	rye	cheese
carrots	turkey	banana	pumpernickel	Swiss cheese
cabbage	tuna	nectarines	crackers	cottage cheese
onion	chicken	kiwi	wheat	yogurt
squash	salmon	apples	spaghetti	milk

Use fats, oils, and sweets sparingly.

Page 69

1. Oahu; 2. Argentina; 3. Mediterranean;
4. Switzerland; 5. Europe; 6. Atlantic;
7. states; 8. Spanish; 9. Western Europe;
10. Mount McKinley; 11. Canada;
12. Australia
to promote world peace

Page 70

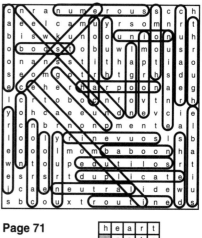

Page 71

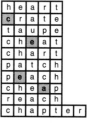

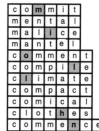

Michelangelo

Page 72

client; constant; slice; stale
continentals

screen; grace; grease; break
greenbacks

danger; garden; regal; tangled
legal tender

Page 73

awful, other, pants, baker, yacht, tower,
pitch; topic, guilt, blend, judge, cable,
paste, loose; sugar, grave, brush, tired,
games, color; helmet; wrist guards;
shoulder pads; goggles; elbow pads;
chest protector; mouth guard; face mask;
shin pads

Page 74

1. endurance; 2. defiance;
3. appearance; 4. resistance;
5. intelligence; 6. acquaintance;
7. ignorance; 8. convenience;
9. guidance; 10. abundance;
11. avoidance; 12. compliance

William Booth founded the Salvation Army. He was born April 10, 1829.

Page 75

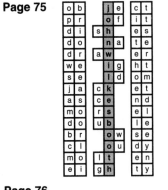

Page 76

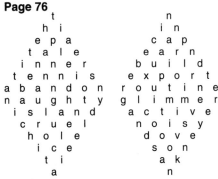

The *Titanic* hit an iceberg and sank.

Page 77

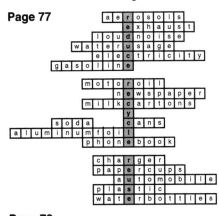

Page 78

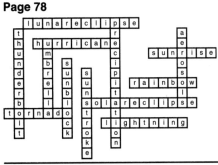

Page 79

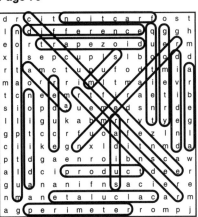

Page 80

The Pony Express Service began.

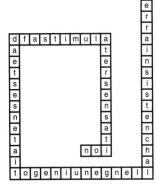

Page 81

1. cell wall; 2. chloroplast; 3. chlorophyll;
4. vascular plant; 5. conifer; 6. ferns;
7. mosses; 8. flowering plants;
9. monocots, dicots

Page 82

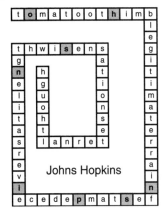

Johns Hopkins

Page 83

Page 84

Page 85

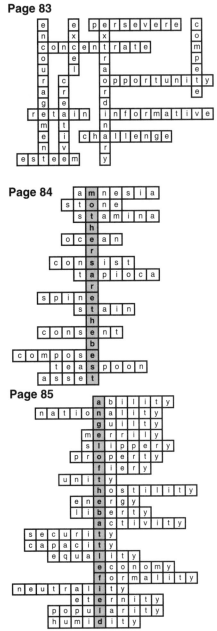

Page 86

exhale; empty; flexible; quiet; before;
healthy; messy; repair; lifted; horizontal;
shallow; stationary; inflate; optimistic;
victory; fatigued; accurate; laugh; dirty;
different
the Empire State Building

Page 87

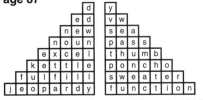

J. F. Kennedy was born on May 29, 1917.